KRAFT
PHILADELPHIA

Cheesecakes & More

WEST SIDE PUBLISHING

Photography on pages 9, 13. 27, 35, 47, 49, 53, 71, 91, 95, 101, 131, 141, 145, 147, 167, 181, 183, 185, 201, 215, 219, 221, 239, 241 and 249 by Kraft Pulse Studio
Photographers: Chris Gould, Mike Egan, and Shannon Moss
Photo Stylists: David Kurth, Randy Martin, and Randy Susick
Prop Stylist: Kathy Lapin
Production Manager: Kristin Clark
Food Stylists: Amy Andrews, Kathy Aragaki, and Carol Parik
Assistant Food Stylists: Shirley Colon, Elaine Funk, and Lisa Knych
Studio Manager: Anna Jenkins
Food Assistant: Simone Gould

Pictured on the front cover: PHILADELPHIA Chocolate-Vanilla Swirl Cheesecake *(page 20)*.

Pictured on the inside front cover: Cream Cheese Flan *(page 48)*.
Pictured on the back cover (clockwise from top): Cucumber Roulades *(page 90)*, Tandoori Chicken Kabobs *(page 166)* and Cinnamon Toast "Blinis" *(page 46), and* Quick Pasta Carbonara *(page 154)*.
Pictured on the inside back cover: Chocolate Ribbon Pie *(page 64)*.

ISBN-13: 978-1-60553-213-4
ISBN-10: 1-60553-213-4

Manufactured in China.

8 7 6 5 4 3 2 1

Nutritional Analysis: Every effort has been made to check the accuracy of the nutritional information that appears with each recipe. However, because numerous variables account for a wide range of values for certain foods, nutritive analyses in this book should be considered approximate. Different results may be obtained by using different nutrient databases and different brand-name products.

Microwave Cooking: Microwave ovens vary in wattage. Use the cooking times as guidelines and check for doneness before adding more time.

Preparation/Cooking Times: Preparation times are based on the approximate amount of time required to assemble the recipe before cooking, baking, chilling, or serving. These times include preparation steps such as measuring, chopping, and mixing. The fact that some preparations and cooking can be done simultaneously is taken into account. Preparation of optional ingredients and serving suggestions is not included.

For consumer inquiries, call Kraft Foods Consumer Helpline 800/431/1001.

contents

4   Tips for the Perfect Cheesecake

6   **Cheesecake Favorites**
An array of timeless family favorites

38   **Everyday Desserts**
Trifles, tortes, oven-free delights and more

64   **Cakes, Cookies & Pies**
Crowd-pleasing treats to enjoy year-round

90   **Make-Ahead Appetizers**
Cold dips and nibbles that can be made in advance

120   **Hot & Savory Appetizers**
Warm and cheesy dips and small bites

146   **Pasta & Casseroles**
Hearty one-dish meals

166   **Entrées**
Easy pork, chicken and seafood dishes

198   **Soups & Sandwiches**
Simple meals made delicious with cream cheese

220   **Side Dishes**
Perfect accompaniments to any meal

250   Index

PHILADELPHIA Cream Cheese Tips for the Perfect Cheesecake

For best quality and results, always use PHILADELPHIA Cream Cheese.

Preheating the oven—The baking time indicated in a recipe is based on using a preheated oven. Turn the oven on when you start to mix the cheesecake ingredients. This should allow enough time for the oven to heat to the correct temperature for when you are ready to place the cheesecake in the oven to bake. Unless otherwise indicated, always bake cheesecakes in the center of the middle oven rack.

Beating the batter—While adding ingredients, do not overbeat the cheesecake batter. Too much air beaten into the batter will result in a cheesecake that sinks in the center when cooled.

Baking cheesecakes—Overbaked cheesecakes tend to crack. Remove cheesecake from oven when center is almost set (i.e. center of cheesecake still wiggles when pan is gently shaken from side-to-side). Although the cheesecake appears underbaked, the residual heat in the cheesecake will be enough to finish baking the center. After chilling, the cheesecake will have a perfectly smooth consistency.

Cooling cheesecakes—Cool cheesecakes completely before refrigerating. Placing a warm cheesecake in the refrigerator will cause condensation to form on the cake, resulting in a soggy cheesecake.

Cutting cheesecakes—Cut cheesecakes when they are cold rather than warm. Use a sharp knife with a clean, thin blade. To make clean cuts, dip the knife in hot water after each cut and wipe the blade clean.

For all of your occasions, PHILLY MAKES A BETTER CHEESECAKE.

During tests of plain New York-style cheesecake made with PHILADELPHIA Cream Cheese versus store-brand versions, consumers rated PHILLY cheesecake as better tasting.

Cheesecake Favorites

An array of timeless family favorites

PHILADELPHIA classic cheesecake

PREP: 20 min. | TOTAL: 5 hours 45 min. (incl. refrigerating) | MAKES: 16 servings.

▶ what you need!

1½ cups HONEY MAID Graham Cracker Crumbs

3 Tbsp. sugar

⅓ cup butter or margarine, melted

4 pkg. (8 oz. each) PHILADELPHIA Cream Cheese, softened

1 cup sugar

1 tsp. vanilla

4 eggs

▶ make it!

HEAT oven to 325°F.

1. **MIX** crumbs, 3 Tbsp. sugar and butter; press onto bottom of 9-inch springform pan.

2. **BEAT** cream cheese, 1 cup sugar and vanilla with mixer until well blended. Add eggs, 1 at a time, mixing on low speed after each just until blended. Pour over crust.

3. **BAKE** 55 min. or until center is almost set. Loosen cake from rim of pan; cool before removing rim. Refrigerate 4 hours.

pumpkin swirl cheesecake

PREP: 20 min. | TOTAL: 5 hours 35 min. (incl. refrigerating) | MAKES: 16 servings.

▶ what you need!

25 NABISCO Ginger Snaps, finely crushed (about 1½ cups)

½ cup finely chopped PLANTERS Pecans

¼ cup (½ stick) butter, melted

4 pkg. (8 oz. each) PHILADELPHIA Cream Cheese, softened

1 cup sugar, divided

1 tsp. vanilla

4 eggs

1 cup canned pumpkin

1 tsp. ground cinnamon

¼ tsp. ground nutmeg

Dash ground cloves

▶ make it!

HEAT oven to 325°F.

1. **LINE** 13×9-inch pan with foil, with ends of foil extending over sides. Mix ginger snap crumbs, nuts and butter; press onto bottom of pan.

2. **BEAT** cream cheese, ¾ cup sugar and vanilla with mixer until well blended. Add eggs, 1 at a time, mixing on low speed after each just until blended. Remove 1½ cups batter; place in small bowl. Stir remaining sugar, pumpkin and spices into remaining batter. Spoon half the pumpkin batter over crust; top with spoonfuls of half the plain batter. Repeat layers; swirl gently with knife.

3. **BAKE** 45 min. or until center is almost set. Cool completely. Refrigerate 4 hours. Use foil handles to lift cheesecake from pan before cutting to serve.

PHILADELPHIA new york-style strawberry swirl cheesecake

PREP: 15 min. | **TOTAL: 5 hours 25 min. (incl. refrigerating)** | **MAKES: 16 servings, 1 piece each.**

▶ what you need!

1 cup HONEY MAID Graham Cracker Crumbs

3 Tbsp. sugar

3 Tbsp. butter, melted

5 pkg. (8 oz. each) PHILADELPHIA Cream Cheese, softened

1 cup sugar

3 Tbsp. flour

1 Tbsp. vanilla

1 cup BREAKSTONE'S or KNUDSEN Sour Cream

4 eggs

⅓ cup seedless strawberry jam

▶ make it!

HEAT oven to 325°F.

1. **LINE** 13×9-inch pan with foil, with ends of foil extending over sides. Mix cracker crumbs, 3 Tbsp. sugar and butter; press onto bottom of pan. Bake 10 min.

2. **BEAT** cream cheese, 1 cup sugar, flour and vanilla in large bowl with mixer until well blended. Add sour cream; mix well. Add eggs, 1 at a time, mixing on low speed after each just until blended. Pour over crust. Gently drop small spoonfuls of jam over batter; swirl with knife.

3. **BAKE** 40 min. or until center is almost set. Cool completely. Refrigerate 4 hours. Use foil handles to lift cheesecake from pan before cutting to serve.

PHILADELPHIA new york-style sour cream-topped cheesecake

PREP: 15 min. | TOTAL: 5 hours 5 min. (incl. refrigerating) | MAKES: 16 servings.

▶ what you need!

1½ cups HONEY MAID Graham Cracker Crumbs

¼ cup (½ stick) butter, melted

1¼ cups sugar, divided

4 pkg. (8 oz. each) PHILADELPHIA Cream Cheese, softened

2 tsp. vanilla, divided

1 container (16 oz.) BREAKSTONE'S or KNUDSEN Sour Cream, divided

4 eggs

2 cups fresh strawberries, sliced

▶ make it!

HEAT oven to 325°F.

1. **LINE** 13×9-inch pan with foil, with ends of foil extending over sides. Mix crumbs, butter and 2 Tbsp. sugar; press onto bottom of pan.

2. **BEAT** cream cheese, 1 cup of the remaining sugar and 1 tsp. vanilla in large bowl with mixer until well blended. Add 1 cup sour cream; mix well. Add eggs, 1 at a time, beating on low speed after each just until blended. Pour over crust.

3. **BAKE** 40 min. or until center is almost set. Mix remaining sour cream, sugar and vanilla; carefully spread over cheesecake. Bake 10 min. Cool completely. Refrigerate 4 hours. Use foil handles to lift cheesecake from pan before cutting to serve; top with berries.

HEALTHY LIVING:
Great news! You'll save 80 calories and 9 grams of fat, including 7 grams of saturated fat, per serving by preparing with PHILADELPHIA Neufchâtel Cheese and BREAKSTONE'S Reduced Fat or KNUDSEN Light Sour Cream.

PHILLY brownie cheesecake

PREP: 10 min. | TOTAL: 6 hours (incl. refrigerating) | MAKES: 16 servings.

▸ what you need!

1 pkg. (19 to 21 oz.) brownie mix (13×9-inch pan size)

4 pkg. (8 oz. each) PHILADELPHIA Cream Cheese, softened

1 cup sugar

1 tsp. vanilla

½ cup BREAKSTONE'S or KNUDSEN Sour Cream

3 eggs

2 squares BAKER'S Semi-Sweet Chocolate

▸ make it!

HEAT oven to 325°F.

1. **PREPARE** brownie batter as directed on package; pour into 13×9-inch pan sprayed with cooking spray. Bake 25 min. or until top is shiny and center is almost set.

2. **MEANWHILE,** beat cream cheese, sugar and vanilla in large bowl with mixer until well blended. Add sour cream; mix well. Add eggs, 1 at a time, mixing on low speed after each just until blended. Gently pour over brownie layer in pan. (Filling will come almost to top of pan.)

3. **BAKE** 40 min. or until center is almost set. Run knife or metal spatula around rim of pan to loosen sides; cool. Refrigerate 4 hours.

4. **MELT** chocolate squares as directed on package; drizzle over cheesecake. Refrigerate 15 min. or until chocolate is firm.

SIZE-WISE:
Balance your food choices throughout the day so you can enjoy a serving of this rich-and-indulgent cheesecake with your loved ones.

fruity cheesecake

PREP: 30 min. | TOTAL: 5 hours 30 min. (incl. refrigerating) | MAKES: 24 servings.

▶ what you need!

60 NILLA Wafers, crushed (about 2 cups)

5 Tbsp. butter or margarine, melted

3 Tbsp. sugar

4 pkg. (8 oz. each) PHILADELPHIA Cream Cheese, softened

1 cup sugar

2 Tbsp. flour

1 cup BREAKSTONE'S or KNUDSEN Sour Cream

4 eggs

1 pkg. (3.4 oz.) JELL-O Lemon Flavor Instant Pudding

2 cups thawed COOL WHIP Whipped Topping

1 cup each blueberries, sliced fresh strawberries and sliced peeled kiwis

▶ make it!

HEAT oven to 325°F.

1. **LINE** 13×9-inch pan with foil, with ends of foil extending over sides. Mix wafer crumbs, butter and 3 Tbsp. sugar; press onto bottom of pan. Bake 10 min.

2. **BEAT** cream cheese, 1 cup sugar and flour in large bowl with mixer until well blended. Add sour cream; mix well. Add eggs, 1 at a time, beating on low speed after each just until blended. Stir in dry pudding mix. Pour over crust.

3. **BAKE** 1 hour or until center of cheesecake is almost set. Cool completely. Refrigerate 4 hours. Use foil handles to lift cheesecake from pan. Remove cheesecake from foil to tray; spread with COOL WHIP. Top with fruit just before serving.

caramel-nut cheesecake

PREP: 20 min. | TOTAL: 5 hours 25 min. (incl. refrigerating) | MAKES: 16 servings.

▶ what you need!

2 cups HONEY MAID Graham Cracker Crumbs

1 cup PLANTERS COCKTAIL Peanuts, chopped, divided

1¼ cups sugar, divided

6 Tbsp. butter or margarine, melted

4 pkg. (8 oz. each) PHILADELPHIA Cream Cheese, softened

2 tsp. vanilla

1 cup BREAKSTONE'S or KNUDSEN Sour Cream

4 eggs

¼ cup caramel ice cream topping

▶ make it!

HEAT oven to 350°F.

1. **LINE** 13×9-inch pan with foil, with ends of foil extending over sides. Mix crumbs, ½ cup nuts, ¼ cup sugar and butter; press onto bottom of pan. Bake 10 min.

2. **MEANWHILE,** beat cream cheese, remaining sugar and vanilla with mixer until well blended. Add sour cream; mix well. Add eggs, 1 at a time, beating after each just until blended. Pour over crust.

3. **BAKE** 35 min. or until center is almost set; cool completely. Refrigerate 4 hours. Top with remaining nuts and caramel topping. Use foil handles to lift cheesecake from pan before cutting to serve.

SPECIAL EXTRA:
Cut chilled cheesecake into 16 bars, then cut each diagonally in half. Stack 2 on each dessert plate to serve.

HOW TO AVOID CRACKED CHEESECAKES:
After adding the eggs, be careful not to overbeat the batter since this can cause the baked cheesecake to crack.

PHILADELPHIA chocolate-vanilla swirl cheesecake

PREP: 15 min. | TOTAL: 5 hours 25 min. (incl. refrigerating) | MAKES: 16 servings.

▸ what you need!

20 OREO Cookies, crushed (about 2 cups)

3 Tbsp. butter, melted

4 pkg. (8 oz. each) PHILADELPHIA Cream Cheese, softened

1 cup sugar

1 tsp. vanilla

1 cup BREAKSTONE'S or KNUDSEN Sour Cream

4 eggs

6 squares BAKER'S Semi-Sweet Chocolate, melted, cooled

▸ make it!

HEAT oven to 325°F.

1. **LINE** 13×9-inch pan with foil, with ends of foil extending over sides. Mix cookie crumbs and butter; press onto bottom of pan. Bake 10 min.

2. **BEAT** cream cheese, sugar and vanilla in large bowl with mixer until well blended. Add sour cream; mix well. Add eggs, 1 at a time, mixing after each just until blended.

3. **RESERVE** 1 cup batter. Stir chocolate into remaining batter; pour over crust. Top with spoonfuls of reserved plain batter; swirl with knife.

4. **BAKE** 40 min. or until center is almost set. Cool. Refrigerate 4 hours. Use foil handles to lift cheesecake from pan before cutting to serve. Garnish with chocolate curls, if desired.

HOW TO MAKE CHOCOLATE CURLS:
Let additional square(s) of BAKER'S Semi-Sweet Chocolate come to room temperature. Carefully draw a vegetable peeler at an angle across the chocolate square to make curls.

PHILADELPHIA
new york cheesecake

PREP: 15 min. | **TOTAL: 5 hours 25 min. (incl. refrigerating)** | **MAKES: 16 servings.**

▶ what you need!

20 OREO Cookies, finely crushed (about 2 cups)

3 Tbsp. butter or margarine, melted

5 pkg. (8 oz. each) PHILADELPHIA Cream Cheese, softened

1 cup sugar

3 Tbsp. flour

1 Tbsp. vanilla

1 cup BREAKSTONE'S or KNUDSEN Sour Cream

4 eggs

1 can (21 oz.) cherry pie filling

▶ make it!

HEAT oven to 325°F.

1.

LINE 13×9-inch pan with foil, with ends of foil extending over sides. Mix crumbs and butter; press onto bottom of pan.

2.

BEAT cream cheese, sugar, flour and vanilla with mixer until well blended. Add sour cream; mix well. Add eggs, 1 at a time, mixing on low speed after each just until blended. Pour over crust.

3.

BAKE 40 min. or until center is almost set. Cool completely. Refrigerate 4 hours. Use foil handles to lift cheesecake from pan before cutting to serve. Top with pie filling.

PHILADELPHIA
double-chocolate cheesecake

PREP: 20 min. | TOTAL: 5 hours 35 min. (incl. refrigerating) | MAKES: 16 servings.

▶ what you need!

24 OREO Cookies, crushed (about 2¼ cups)

¼ cup (½ stick) butter or margarine, melted

4 pkg. (8 oz. each) PHILADELPHIA Cream Cheese, softened

1 cup sugar

2 Tbsp. flour

1 tsp. vanilla

1 pkg. (8 squares) BAKER'S Semi-Sweet Chocolate, melted, slightly cooled

4 eggs

▶ make it!

HEAT oven to 325°F.

1. **LINE** 13×9-inch pan with foil, with ends of foil extending over sides. Mix crumbs and butter; press onto bottom of pan. Bake 10 min.

2. **BEAT** cream cheese, sugar, flour and vanilla with mixer until well blended. Add chocolate; mix well. Add eggs, 1 at a time, mixing on low speed after each just until blended. Pour over crust.

3. **BAKE** 45 min. or until center is almost set. Cool completely. Refrigerate 4 hours. Use foil handles to lift cheesecake from pan before cutting to serve.

SPECIAL EXTRA:
Garnish with sifted powdered sugar and mixed berries just before serving.

ultimate turtle cheesecake

PREP: 30 min. | TOTAL: 6 hours 10 min. (incl. refrigerating) | MAKES: 16 servings.

▶ what you need!

2 cups OREO Chocolate Cookie Crumbs

6 Tbsp. butter or margarine, melted

1 pkg. (14 oz.) KRAFT Caramels

½ cup milk

1 cup chopped PLANTERS Pecans

3 pkg. (8 oz. each) PHILADELPHIA Cream Cheese, softened

¾ cup sugar

1 Tbsp. vanilla

3 eggs

2 squares BAKER'S Semi-Sweet Chocolate

▶ make it!

HEAT oven to 325°F.

1. **MIX** crumbs and butter; press onto bottom and 2 inches up side of 9-inch springform pan.

2. **MICROWAVE** caramels and milk in small microwaveable bowl on HIGH 3 min. or until caramels are completely melted, stirring after each minute. Stir in nuts; pour half into crust. Refrigerate 10 min. Refrigerate remaining caramel mixture for later use.

3. **BEAT** cream cheese, sugar and vanilla with mixer until well blended. Add eggs, 1 at a time, mixing on low speed after each just until blended. Pour over caramel layer in crust.

4. **BAKE** 1 hour 5 min. to 1 hour 10 min. or until center is almost set. Run knife around rim of pan to loosen cake; cool before removing rim. Refrigerate 4 hours.

5. **MICROWAVE** reserved caramel mixture 1 min.; stir. Pour over cheesecake. Melt chocolate as directed on package; drizzle over cheesecake.

chocolate bliss cheesecake

PREP: 20 min. | **TOTAL:** 6 hours (incl. refrigerating) | **MAKES:** 12 servings.

▸ what you need!

18 OREO Cookies, finely crushed (about 1¾ cups)

2 Tbsp. butter or margarine, melted

3 pkg. (8 oz. each) PHILADELPHIA Cream Cheese, softened

¾ cup sugar

1 tsp. vanilla

1 pkg. (8 squares) BAKER'S Semi-Sweet Chocolate, melted, cooled slightly

3 eggs

▸ make it!

HEAT oven to 325°F.

1.

MIX crumbs and butter; press onto bottom of 9-inch springform pan.

2.

BEAT cream cheese, sugar and vanilla with mixer until well blended. Add chocolate; mix well. Add eggs, 1 at a time, mixing on low speed after each just until blended. Pour over crust.

3.

BAKE 55 min. to 1 hour or until center is almost set. Run knife around rim of pan to loosen cake; cool before removing rim. Refrigerate 4 hours. Garnish with powdered sugar and fresh raspberries just before serving, if desired.

lemon pudding cheesecake

PREP: 15 min. | TOTAL: 6 hours (incl. refrigerating) | MAKES: 16 servings.

▶ what you need!

40 NILLA Wafers, crushed (about 1½ cups)

¾ cup plus 1 Tbsp. sugar, divided

3 Tbsp. butter or margarine, melted

4 pkg. (8 oz. each) PHILADELPHIA Cream Cheese, softened

2 Tbsp. flour

2 Tbsp. milk

1 cup BREAKSTONE'S or KNUDSEN Sour Cream

2 pkg. (3.4 oz. each) JELL-O Lemon Flavor Instant Pudding

4 eggs

1 cup thawed COOL WHIP Strawberry Whipped Topping

2 squares BAKER'S White Chocolate

▶ make it!

HEAT oven to 325°F.

1. **MIX** wafer crumbs, 1 Tbsp. sugar and butter; press firmly onto bottom of 9-inch springform pan. Bake 10 min.

2. **BEAT** cream cheese, remaining sugar, flour and milk with mixer until well blended. Add sour cream; mix well. Blend in dry pudding mixes. Add eggs, 1 at a time, mixing on low speed after each just until blended.

3. **BAKE** 1 hour 5 min. to 1 hour 15 min. or until center is almost set. Run knife around rim of pan to loosen cake; cool before removing rim. Refrigerate 4 hours. Meanwhile, prepare chocolate curls from white chocolate. Top cheesecake with COOL WHIP and chocolate curls just before serving.

HOW TO MAKE CHOCOLATE CURLS:
Melt chocolate as directed on package. Spread with spatula into very thin layer on baking sheet. Refrigerate 10 mins., or until firm but still pliable. To make curls, push a metal spatula firmly along the baking sheet, under the chocolate, so the chocolate curls as it is pushed. (If chocolate is too firm to curl, let stand a few minutes at room temperature; refrigerate again if it becomes too soft.) Use toothpick to carefully place chocolate curls on wax paper-covered tray. Refrigerate 15 mins. or until firm. Use toothpick to arrange curls on dessert.

scrumptious apple-pecan cheesecake

PREP: 25 min. | TOTAL: 6 hours 10 min. (incl. refrigerating) | MAKES: 12 servings.

▶ what you need!

1 cup HONEY MAID Graham Cracker Crumbs

¾ cup finely chopped PLANTERS Pecans, divided

3 Tbsp. sugar

1 tsp. ground cinnamon, divided

¼ cup (½ stick) butter or margarine, melted

2 pkg. (8 oz. each) PHILADELPHIA Cream Cheese, softened

½ cup sugar

½ tsp. vanilla

2 eggs

⅓ cup sugar

4 cups thin peeled apple slices

▶ make it!

HEAT oven to 325°F.

1. **MIX** crumbs, ½ cup nuts, 3 Tbsp. sugar, ½ tsp. cinnamon and butter; press onto bottom of 9-inch springform pan. Bake 10 min.

2. **BEAT** cream cheese, ½ cup sugar and vanilla with mixer until well blended. Add eggs, 1 at a time, beating on low speed after each just until blended. Pour over crust. Mix ⅓ cup sugar and remaining cinnamon in large bowl. Add apples; toss to coat. Spoon over cream cheese layer; sprinkle with remaining nuts.

3. **BAKE** 1 hour 10 min. to 1 hour 15 min. or until center is almost set. Run knife around rim of pan to loosen cake; cool before removing rim. Refrigerate 4 hours.

cappuccino cheesecake

PREP: 25 min. | TOTAL: 6 hours 5 min. (incl. refrigerating) | MAKES: 16 servings.

▶ what you need!

1½ cups finely chopped PLANTERS Walnuts

3 Tbsp. butter or margarine, melted

2 Tbsp. sugar

4 pkg. (8 oz. each) PHILADELPHIA Cream Cheese, softened

1 cup sugar

3 Tbsp. flour

4 eggs

1 cup BREAKSTONE'S or KNUDSEN Sour Cream

1 Tbsp. MAXWELL HOUSE Instant Coffee

¼ tsp. ground cinnamon

¼ cup boiling water

1½ cups thawed COOL WHIP Whipped Topping

▶ make it!

HEAT oven to 325°F.

1. **MIX** nuts, butter and 2 Tbsp. sugar; press onto bottom of 9-inch springform pan. Bake 10 min. Remove from oven; cool. Increase oven temperature to 450°F.

2. **BEAT** cream cheese, 1 cup sugar and flour with mixer until well blended. Add eggs, 1 at a time, mixing on low speed after each just until blended. Blend in sour cream.

3. **DISSOLVE** instant coffee with cinnamon in water; cool. Gradually add to cream cheese mixture, mixing until well blended. Pour over crust.

4. **BAKE** 10 min. Reduce oven temperature to 250°F. Bake an additional 1 hour or until center is almost set. Run knife around rim of pan to loosen cake, cool before removing rim. Refrigerate 4 hours. Top with dollops of COOL WHIP. Garnish with a sprinkle of additional cinnamon, if desired.

OREO chocolate cheesecake

PREP: 30 min. | **TOTAL: 5 hours 45 min. (incl. refrigerating)** | **MAKES: 14 servings.**

▶ what you need!

38 OREO Cookies, divided

5 Tbsp. butter or margarine, melted

5 squares BAKER'S Semi-Sweet Chocolate, divided

1 pkg. (8 oz.) PHILADELPHIA Cream Cheese, softened

½ cup plus 2 Tbsp. sugar, divided

1½ cups BREAKSTONE'S or KNUDSEN Sour Cream, divided

1 tsp. vanilla

2 eggs

▶ make it!

HEAT oven to 325°F.

1. **CRUSH** 24 cookies; mix with butter. Press onto bottom of 9-inch springform pan. Stand remaining cookies around inside edge of pan, firmly pressing bottom edge of each cookie into crust.

2. **MELT** 4 chocolate squares as directed on package. Beat cream cheese and ½ cup sugar with mixer until well blended. Add ½ cup sour cream, vanilla and chocolate; mix well. Add eggs, 1 at a time, mixing on low speed after each just until blended. Pour over crust.

3. **BAKE** 35 to 40 min. or until center is almost set. Mix remaining sour cream and sugar; spread over cheesecake. Bake 5 min. Run knife around rim of pan to loosen cake; cool before removing rim.

4. **MELT** remaining chocolate square; drizzle over cheesecake. Refrigerate 4 hours.

SPECIAL EXTRA:
Garnish as desired.

Everyday Desserts

Trifles, tortes, oven-free delights and more

strawberry freeze

PREP: 15 min. plus freezing | MAKES: 16 servings.

▶ what you need!

12 CHIPS AHOY! Cookies

1 pkg. (8 oz.) PHILADELPHIA Cream Cheese, softened

½ cup sugar

1 can (12 oz.) frozen berry juice concentrate, thawed

1 cup crushed strawberries

1 tub (8 oz.) COOL WHIP Whipped Topping, thawed

2 cups whole strawberries, cut in half

▶ make it!

1. **ARRANGE** cookies in single layer on bottom of 9-inch springform pan.

2. **BEAT** cream cheese and sugar with mixer until well blended. Gradually beat in juice concentrate. Stir in crushed strawberries. Whisk in COOL WHIP until well blended. Pour over cookies in pan.

3. **FREEZE** 6 hours or until firm. Remove from freezer 15 min. before serving; let stand at room temperature to soften slightly. Top with berry halves just before serving.

SUBSTITUTE:
Prepare using COOL WHIP Strawbery Whipped Topping.

banana split cake

PREP: 15 min. plus refrigerating | MAKES: 24 servings.

▶ what you need!

9 HONEY MAID Honey Grahams, crushed (about 1½ cups)

1 cup sugar, divided

⅓ cup butter, melted

2 pkg. (8 oz. each) PHILADELPHIA Cream Cheese, softened

1 can (20 oz.) crushed pineapple, in juice, drained

6 bananas, divided

2 pkg. (3.4 oz. each) JELL-O Vanilla Flavor Instant Pudding

2 cups cold milk

2 cups thawed COOL WHIP Whipped Topping, divided

1 cup chopped PLANTERS Pecans

▶ make it!

1. **MIX** crumbs, ¼ cup sugar and butter; press onto bottom of 13×9-inch pan. Freeze 10 min.

2. **BEAT** cream cheese and remaining sugar with mixer until well blended. Spread carefully over crust; top with pineapple. Slice 4 bananas; arrange over pineapple.

3. **BEAT** pudding mixes and milk with whisk 2 min. Stir in 1 cup COOL WHIP; spread over banana layer in pan. Top with remaining COOL WHIP. Refrigerate 5 hours. Slice remaining 2 bananas just before serving; arrange over dessert. Top with nuts.

SIZE-WISE:
This banana split-inspired dessert makes a great treat to share with friends and family.

striped delight

PREP: 20 min. | TOTAL: 4 hours 40 min. (incl. refrigerating) | MAKES: 24 servings.

▶ what you need!

35 OREO Cookies

6 Tbsp. butter, melted

1 pkg. (8 oz.) PHILADELPHIA Cream Cheese, softened

¼ cup sugar

2 Tbsp. cold milk

1 tub (12 oz.) COOL WHIP Whipped Topping, thawed, divided

2 pkg. (3.9 oz. each) JELL-O Chocolate Instant Pudding

3¼ cups cold milk

▶ make it!

1. **PROCESS** cookies in food processor until fine crumbs form. Transfer to medium bowl; mix in butter. Press onto bottom of 13×9-inch dish. Refrigerate until ready to use.

2. **WHISK** cream cheese, sugar and 2 Tbsp. milk in medium bowl until blended. Stir in 1¼ cups COOL WHIP; spread over crust.

3. **BEAT** pudding mixes and 3¼ cups milk with whisk 2 min.; pour over cream cheese layer. Let stand 5 min. or until thickened; cover with remaining COOL WHIP. Refrigerate 4 hours.

SIZE-WISE:
Enjoy this dessert on a special occasion, but stick to the serving size of this rich treat.

HOW TO EASILY CUT INTO SQUARES:
Place dessert in freezer about 1 hour before cutting into squares to serve.

SPECIAL EXTRA:
Drizzle each plate with melted BAKER'S Semi-Sweet Chocolate before topping with dessert square. Sprinkle with crushed candy canes or additional crushed OREO Cookies.

chocolate & peanut butter ribbon dessert

PREP: 15 min. plus freezing | MAKES: 12 servings.

▶ what you need!

12 NUTTER BUTTER Peanut Butter Sandwich Cookies, divided

2 Tbsp. butter, melted

1 pkg. (8 oz.) PHILADELPHIA Cream Cheese, softened

½ cup creamy peanut butter

½ cup sugar

2 tsp. vanilla

1 tub (12 oz.) COOL WHIP Whipped Topping, thawed, divided

2 squares BAKER'S Semi-Sweet Chocolate, melted

▶ make it!

1. **CRUSH** 8 cookies; mix with butter. Press onto bottom of foil-lined 9×5-inch loaf pan.

2. **MIX** next 4 ingredients with mixer until well blended. Whisk in 3 cups COOL WHIP; spoon ½ cup into small bowl. Blend in melted chocolate. Spoon half the remaining cream cheese mixture over crust; top with layers of chocolate mixture and remaining cream cheese mixture.

3. **FREEZE** 4 hours or until firm. Invert onto plate. Remove foil, then re-invert dessert onto serving platter so crumb layer is on bottom. Coarsely break remaining cookies. Top dessert with remaining COOL WHIP and cookies.

SIZE-WISE:
Savor a serving of this indulgent special-occasion dessert. One loaf makes enough for 12 servings.

MAKE AHEAD:
Dessert can be frozen overnight before unmolding and serving as directed.

cinnamon toast "blinis"

PREP: 20 min. | TOTAL: 35 min. | MAKES: 18 servings.

▸ what you need!

1 pkg. (8 oz.) PHILADELPHIA Cream Cheese, softened

½ cup sugar, divided

¼ tsp. vanilla

1 egg yolk

1 tsp. ground cinnamon

12 slices white bread, crusts removed

3 Tbsp. butter or margarine, melted

▸ make it!

HEAT oven to 400°F.

1. **BEAT** cream cheese, ¼ cup sugar, vanilla and egg yolk with whisk until well blended. In separate bowl, mix remaining sugar and cinnamon.

2. **FLATTEN** bread slices with rolling pin. Spread each with 1 rounded Tbsp. cream cheese mixture; roll up tightly, starting at 1 short end. Brush with butter; roll in reserved cinnamon sugar. Cut each roll into 3 pieces; place, seam-sides down, on baking sheet.

3. **BAKE** 12 to 15 min. or until edges are lightly browned. Serve warm.

Rolls can be prepared ahead of time and kept frozen until ready to slice and bake.

cream cheese flan

PREP: 20 min. | TOTAL: 4 hours 50 min. (incl. refrigerating) | MAKES: 8 servings.

▶ what you need!

2 cups sugar, divided

1 can (12 oz.) evaporated milk

1 pkg. (8 oz.) PHILADELPHIA Cream Cheese, cubed, softened

5 eggs

1 tsp. vanilla

Dash salt

▶ make it!

HEAT oven to 350°F.

1. **COOK** 1 cup sugar in small saucepan on medium heat until sugar is melted and deep golden brown, stirring constantly. Pour into 9-inch round pan; tilt pan to cover bottom with syrup.

2. **BLEND** milk and cream cheese in blender until smooth. Add remaining sugar, eggs, vanilla and salt; blend just until smooth. Pour over syrup in pan. Place filled pan in larger pan; add enough hot water to larger pan to come halfway up side of smaller pan.

3. **BAKE** 50 min. to 1 hour or until knife inserted near center comes out clean. Cool slightly. Carefully remove flan from water. Cool completely on wire rack. Refrigerate several hours or until chilled. Unmold onto plate just before serving.

FLAVOR VARIATIONS:
Prepare as directed. Choose one of the following options: **Guava:** Add ½ cup guava paste, cut into pieces, or ½ cup canned guava shells in heavy syrup to cream cheese batter before pouring into prepared pan. **Lime:** Add zest from 1 lime to boiling sugar mixture; remove from syrup before sugar caramelizes. Pour into prepared pan as directed. **Cajeta:** Add ¼ cup cajeta (Mexican goat milk caramel) to cream cheese batter before pouring into prepared pan. **Chocolate-Orange:** Add 2 squares BAKER'S Semi-Sweet Chocolate, melted and cooled, and 1 Tbsp. orange zest to cream cheese batter before pouring into prepared pan. **Coconut:** Omit vanilla and add ¼ cup BAKER'S ANGEL FLAKE Coconut or ½ cup coconut milk and 1 Tbsp. rum to cream cheese batter before pouring into prepared pan.

SPECIAL EXTRA:
Garnish with fresh berries just before serving.

layered strawberry cheesecake bowl

PREP: 20 min. plus refrigerating | MAKES: 14 servings, ⅔ cup each.

▶ what you need!

3 cups sliced fresh strawberries

3 Tbsp. sugar

2 pkg. (8 oz. each) PHILADELPHIA Neufchâtel Cheese, softened

1½ cups cold milk

1 pkg. (3.4 oz.) JELL-O Vanilla Flavor Instant Pudding

2 cups thawed COOL WHIP LITE Whipped Topping, divided

2 cups frozen pound cake cubes (1 inch)

1 square BAKER'S Semi-Sweet Chocolate

▶ make it!

1. **COMBINE** berries and sugar; refrigerate until ready to use. Beat Neufchâtel with mixer until creamy. Gradually beat in milk. Add dry pudding mix; mix well.

2. **BLEND** in 1½ cups COOL WHIP. Spoon half into 2½-qt. bowl.

3. **TOP** with layers of cake, berries and remaining Neufchâtel mixture. Refrigerate 4 hours.

4. **MELT** chocolate; drizzle over trifle. Top with remaining COOL WHIP.

SPECIAL EXTRA:
Garnish with chocolate-covered strawberries just before serving.

NOTE:
You will need about half of a 10.75-oz. pkg. pound cake to get the 4 cups cake cubes needed to prepare this recipe.

white chocolate-raspberry torte

PREP: 20 min. plus refrigerating | MAKES: 12 servings.

▶ what you need!

4 squares BAKER'S White Chocolate, melted

1 pkg. (8 oz.) PHILADELPHIA Cream Cheese, softened

1 cup cold milk

1 pkg. (3.4 oz.) JELL-O Vanilla Flavor Instant Pudding

2 cups thawed COOL WHIP Whipped Topping, divided

1 pkg. (10.5 oz.) frozen pound cake, partially thawed, cut into 30 thin slices

¼ cup raspberry jam, warmed

½ cup fresh raspberries

▶ make it!

1. **BEAT** chocolate and cream cheese with mixer until blended. Gradually beat in milk. Add dry pudding mix; beat until well blended. Whisk in 1 cup COOL WHIP.

2. **ARRANGE** 10 cake slices on bottom of 9-inch round pan lined with plastic wrap; brush with half the jam.

3. **COVER** with half the pudding mixture. Repeat all layers. Top with remaining cake.

4. **REFRIGERATE** 3 hours. Invert dessert onto plate; remove pan and plastic wrap. Top with remaining COOL WHIP and berries.

SIZE-WISE:
Balance your food choices during the day so you can treat yourself to a serving of this luscious raspberry dessert.

VARIATION:
Prepare using BAKER'S Semi-Sweet Chocolate and JELL-O Chocolate Instant Pudding, and adding ½ cup more COOL WHIP to the pudding mixture before using as directed.

chocolate mousse torte

PREP: 20 min. plus refrigerating | MAKES: 16 servings.

▶ what you need!

37 NILLA Wafers, divided

4 squares BAKER'S Semi-Sweet Chocolate, divided

2 pkg. (3.9 oz. each) JELL-O Chocolate Instant Pudding

2 cups plus 2 Tbsp. cold milk, divided

1 tub (8 oz.) COOL WHIP Whipped Topping, thawed, divided

1 pkg. (8 oz.) PHILADELPHIA Cream Cheese, softened

¼ cup sugar

¾ cup fresh raspberries

▶ make it!

1.  **STAND** 16 wafers around inside edge of 9-inch round pan lined with plastic wrap. Melt 3 chocolate squares as directed on package.

2.  **BEAT** pudding mixes and 2 cups milk with whisk 2 min. Add melted chocolate; mix well. Stir in 1 cup COOL WHIP; pour into prepared pan. Beat cream cheese, sugar and remaining milk with mixer until well blended.

3.  **STIR** in 1 cup of the remaining COOL WHIP; spread over pudding. Top with remaining wafers. Refrigerate 3 hours.

4.  **MEANWHILE,** shave remaining chocolate square into curls. Invert torte onto plate. Remove pan and plastic wrap. Top torte with remaining COOL WHIP, berries and chocolate curls.

fast & easy tiramisu

PREP: 15 min. plus refrigerating | MAKES: 12 servings.

▶ what you need!

- 2 pkg. (3 oz. each) ladyfingers, split, divided
- 2 Tbsp. MAXWELL HOUSE Instant Coffee
- 1 Tbsp. sugar
- 1 cup boiling water
- 2 pkg. (8 oz. each) PHILADELPHIA Fat Free Cream Cheese, softened
- ½ cup sugar
- 2 cups thawed COOL WHIP LITE Whipped Topping
- 1 tsp. unsweetened cocoa powder

▶ make it!

1. **ARRANGE** 1 package of ladyfingers on bottom of 13×9-inch baking dish. Dissolve combined coffee granules and 1 Tbsp. sugar in boiling water; brush ½ cup onto ladyfingers in dish.

2. **BEAT** cream cheese in large bowl with mixer until creamy. Add ½ cup sugar; mix well. Whisk in COOL WHIP.

3. **SPREAD** half the cream cheese mixture over ladyfingers in dish; top with remaining ladyfingers. Brush with remaining coffee mixture; cover with remaining cream cheese mixture. Sprinkle with cocoa powder. Refrigerate 4 hours.

SPECIAL EXTRA:
Add 2 Tbsp. almond-flavored liqueur or brandy to cream cheese along with the ½ cup sugar.

NUTRITION BONUS:
This tasty variation of a classic dessert provides calcium from the cream cheese.

PHILADELPHIA "fruit smoothie" no-bake cheesecake

PREP: 15 min. plus refrigerating | MAKES: 16 servings.

▶ what you need!

2 cups HONEY MAID Graham Cracker Crumbs

6 Tbsp. butter, melted

3 Tbsp. sugar

4 pkg. (8 oz. each) PHILADELPHIA Neufchâtel Cheese, softened

¾ cup sugar

1 pkg. (12 oz.) frozen mixed berries (strawberries, raspberries, blueberries and blackberries), thawed, well drained

1 tub (8 oz.) COOL WHIP LITE Whipped Topping, thawed

▶ make it!

1. **LINE** 13×9-inch pan with foil, with ends of foil extending over sides. Mix crumbs, butter and 3 Tbsp. sugar; press onto bottom of pan. Refrigerate while preparing filling.

2. **BEAT** Neufchâtel and ¾ cup sugar with mixer until well blended. Add berries; beat on low speed just until blended. Whisk in COOL WHIP. Pour over crust.

3. **REFRIGERATE** 4 hours or until firm. Use foil handles to lift cheesecake from pan before cutting to serve.

SPECIAL EXTRA:
Garnish with fresh berries just before serving.

VARIATION.
Prepare as directed, substituting 3 cups mixed fresh berries for the package of frozen berries and increasing the sugar mixed with the Neufchâtel mixture to 1 cup.

rocky road no-bake cheesecake

PREP: 15 min. plus refrigerating | MAKES: 10 servings.

▶ what you need!

3 squares BAKER'S Semi-Sweet Chocolate, divided

2 pkg. (8 oz. each) PHILADELPHIA Cream Cheese, softened

⅓ cup sugar

¼ cup milk

2 cups thawed COOL WHIP Whipped Topping

¾ cup JET-PUFFED Miniature Marshmallows

⅓ cup chopped PLANTERS COCKTAIL Peanuts

1 OREO Pie Crust (6 oz.)

▶ make it!

1. **MICROWAVE** 1 chocolate square as directed on package. Coarsely chop remaining chocolate squares.

2. **BEAT** cream cheese, sugar and milk with mixer until well blended. Add melted chocolate; mix well. Whisk in COOL WHIP until well blended. Stir in chopped chocolate, marshmallows and nuts. Pour into crust.

3. **REFRIGERATE** 4 hours or until set.

SIZE-WISE:
Since this indulgent cheesecake makes 10 servings, it's the perfect dessert to serve at your next party.

SPECIAL EXTRA:
Shave 1 additional chocolate square. Use to garnish dessert along with additional marshmallows.

PHILADELPHIA peaches 'n cream no-bake cheesecake

PREP: 15 min. plus refrigerating | MAKES: 16 servings.

▶ what you need!

2 cups HONEY MAID Graham Cracker Crumbs

6 Tbsp. margarine, melted

1 cup sugar, divided

4 pkg. (8 oz. each) PHILADELPHIA Neufchâtel Cheese, softened

1 pkg. (3 oz.) JELL-O Peach Flavor Gelatin

2 fresh peaches, chopped

1 tub (8 oz.) COOL WHIP LITE Whipped Topping, thawed

▶ make it!

1. **MIX** graham crumbs, margarine and ¼ cup sugar; press onto bottom of 13×9-inch pan. Refrigerate while preparing filling.

2. **BEAT** Neufchâtel and remaining sugar with mixer until well blended. Add dry gelatin mix; mix well. Stir in peaches and COOL WHIP; spread onto bottom of crust.

3. **REFRIGERATE** 4 hours or until firm.

SIZE-WISE:
You'll know it is a special occasion when you get to enjoy a serving of this luscious cheesecake.

SUBSTITUTE:
Prepare using 1 drained 15-oz. can peaches.

Cakes, Cookies & Pies

Crowd-pleasing treats to enjoy year-round

chocolate ribbon pie

PREP: 15 min. plus refrigerating | MAKES: 8 servings.

▶ what you need!

4 oz. (½ of 8-oz. pkg.) PHILADELPHIA Cream Cheese, softened

2 Tbsp. sugar

2 cups plus 1 Tbsp. milk, divided

1 tub (8 oz.) COOL WHIP Whipped Topping, thawed, divided

1 OREO Pie Crust (6 oz.)

2 pkg. (3.9 oz. each) JELL-O Chocolate Instant Pudding

▶ make it!

1. **BEAT** cream cheese, sugar and 1 Tbsp. milk in medium bowl with whisk until well blended. Stir in half the COOL WHIP; spread onto bottom of crust.

2. **BEAT** pudding mixes and remaining milk with whisk 2 min. (Mixture will be thick.) Pour over layer in crust.

3. **REFRIGERATE** 4 hours or until firm. Top with remaining COOL WHIP just before serving.

HOW TO SOFTEN CREAM CHEESE:
Place measured amount of cream cheese on microwaveable plate. Microwave on HIGH 10 sec. or until slightly softened.

shortcut carrot cake

PREP: 30 min. | TOTAL: 1 hour 30 min. (incl. cooking) | MAKES: 18 servings.

▶ what you need!

1 pkg. (2-layer size) spice cake mix

2 cups shredded carrots (about 3 large)

1 can (8 oz.) crushed pineapple, drained

1 cup chopped PLANTERS Pecans, divided

2 pkg. (8 oz. each) PHILADELPHIA Cream Cheese, softened

2 cups powdered sugar

1 tub (8 oz.) COOL WHIP Whipped Topping, thawed

▶ make it!

HEAT oven to 350°F.

1. **PREPARE** cake batter as directed on package; stir in carrots, pineapple and ¾ cup nuts. Pour into 2 (9-inch) square pans. Bake 25 to 30 min. or until toothpick inserted in centers comes out clean. Cool in pans 10 min.; invert onto wire racks. Remove pans. Turn cakes over; cool completely.

2. **MEANWHILE,** beat cream cheese and sugar until well blended. Whisk in COOL WHIP.

3. **STACK** cake layers on plate, spreading frosting between layers and on top and sides of cake. Top with remaining nuts. Keep refrigerated.

SIZE-WISE:
Looking for a simple dessert to serve at a party? This quick version of a classic serves 18 people.

FOR A DECORATIVE DESIGN:
Use a toothpick to draw 4 diagonal lines across top of cake; sprinkle remaining ¼ cup nuts over lines.

SUBSTITUTE:
Substitute a yellow cake mix plus 2 tsp. ground cinnamon for the spice cake mix.

banana-sour cream cake

PREP: 15 min. | TOTAL: 1 hour 50 min. (incl. cooling) | MAKES: 16 servings.

▶ what you need!

1 pkg. (2-layer size) yellow cake mix

3 eggs

1 cup mashed ripe bananas (about 3)

1 cup BREAKSTONE'S or KNUDSEN Sour Cream

¼ cup oil

1 pkg. (8 oz.) PHILADELPHIA Cream Cheese, softened

½ cup (1 stick) butter, softened

1 pkg. (16 oz.) powdered sugar

1 cup finely chopped PLANTERS Walnuts

▶ make it!

HEAT oven to 350°F.

1. **BEAT** first 5 ingredients with mixer on low speed just until moistened, stopping frequently to scrape bottom and side of bowl. Beat on medium speed 2 min. Pour into greased and floured 13×9-inch pan.

2. **BAKE** 35 min. or until toothpick inserted in center comes out clean. Cool completely.

3. **BEAT** cream cheese and butter with mixer until well blended. Gradually add sugar, beating well after each addition.

4. **REMOVE** cake from pan. Carefully cut cake crosswise in half using serrated knife. Place 1 cake half, top-side down, on plate; spread with some of the cream cheese frosting. Top with remaining cake half, top-side up. Spread top and sides with remaining frosting. Press nuts into sides. Keep refrigerated.

SUBSTITUTE:
Prepare using BREAKSTONE'S Reduced Fat or KNUDSEN Light Sour Cream.

grandma's pound cake

PREP: 15 min. | TOTAL: 1 hour 15 min. | MAKES: 12 servings.

▸ what you need!

1 cup (2 sticks) butter, softened

2 cups sugar

1 pkg. (8 oz.) PHILADELPHIA Cream Cheese, cubed, softened

1 tsp. vanilla

6 eggs

2 cups flour

1 Tbsp. CALUMET Baking Powder

1 tsp. salt

▸ make it!

HEAT oven to 350°F.

1. **BEAT** butter in large bowl with mixer 1 min. Gradually beat in sugar. Beat 5 min. or until light and fluffy. Add cream cheese and vanilla; beat 1 min. Beat in eggs, 1 at a time.

2. **MIX** flour, baking powder and salt. Add to butter mixture. Beat 1 min. or until well blended. Pour into greased and floured 12-cup fluted tube or 10-inch tube pan.

3. **BAKE** 1 hour or until toothpick inserted near center comes out clean. Cool in pan 10 min. Loosen cake from side of pan with knife. Invert cake onto wire rack; gently remove pan. Cool cake completely.

SIZE-WISE:
This indulgent special-occasion cake is a perfect dessert to serve at your next party. One cake makes enough for 12 servings.

SPECIAL EXTRA:
Serve the pound cake with fresh berries (strawberries, raspberries or blueberries); top with a dollop of thawed COOL WHIP Whipped Topping or your favorite ice cream.

berry-berry cake

PREP: 25 min. | TOTAL: 2 hours (incl. cooling) | MAKES: 12 servings.

► what you need!

⅓ cup PHILADELPHIA ⅓ Less Fat than Cream Cheese

¾ cup sugar, divided

2 egg whites

2 tsp. lemon zest

1 cup plus 2 tsp. flour, divided

½ tsp. baking soda

⅓ cup BREAKSTONE'S FREE or KNUDSEN FREE Fat Free Sour Cream

3 cups mixed fresh blueberries and raspberries, divided

► make it!

HEAT oven to 350°F.

1. **BEAT** reduced-fat cream cheese and ½ cup sugar in large bowl with mixer until well blended. Add egg whites and zest; mix well. Mix 1 cup flour and baking soda. Add to cream cheese mixture alternately with sour cream, beating well after each addition. (Do not overmix.)

2. **SPREAD** onto bottom and 1 inch up side of 9-inch springform pan sprayed with cooking spray. Toss 2 cups berries with remaining sugar and flour; spoon over cream cheese mixture in bottom of pan to within ½ inch of edge.

3. **BAKE** 40 to 45 min. or until toothpick inserted in center comes out clean. Run knife around rim of pan to loosen cake; cool before removing rim. Top cake with remaining berries. Keep refrigerated.

NUTRITION BONUS:
Take advantage of seasonal fresh berries when making this elegant low-fat cake.

red velvet cupcakes

PREP: 15 min. | TOTAL: 1 hour 10 min. (incl. cooling) | MAKES: 24 servings.

▸ what you need!

1 pkg. (2-layer size) red velvet cake mix

1 pkg. (3.9 oz.) JELL-O Chocolate Instant Pudding

1 pkg. (8 oz.) PHILADELPHIA Cream Cheese, softened

½ cup (1 stick) butter or margarine, softened

1 pkg. (16 oz.) powdered sugar (about 4 cups)

1 cup thawed COOL WHIP Whipped Topping

1 square BAKER'S White Chocolate, shaved into curls

▸ make it!

1.

PREPARE cake batter and bake as directed on package for 24 cupcakes, blending dry pudding mix into batter before spooning into prepared muffin cups. Cool.

2.

MEANWHILE, beat cream cheese and butter in large bowl with mixer until well blended. Gradually beat in sugar. Whisk in COOL WHIP; spoon 1½ cups into resealable plastic bag. Seal bag; cut 1 small corner off bottom of bag. Use to squeeze 1 Tbsp. cream cheese frosting into center of each cupcake.

3.

FROST cupcakes with remaining frosting. Top with chocolate curls. Keep refrigerated.

creamy lemon squares

PREP: 25 min. | TOTAL: 3 hours 23 min. (incl. refrigerating) | MAKES: 16 servings.

▶ what you need!

20 Reduced Fat NILLA Wafers, finely crushed
   (about ¾ cup)

½ cup flour

¼ cup packed brown sugar

¼ cup (½ stick) cold margarine

1 pkg. (8 oz.) PHILADELPHIA Neufchâtel
   Cheese, softened

1 cup granulated sugar

2 eggs

2 Tbsp. flour

1 Tbsp. lemon zest

¼ cup fresh lemon juice

¼ tsp. CALUMET Baking Powder

2 tsp. powdered sugar

▶ make it!

HEAT oven to 350°F.

1. **LINE** 8-inch square pan with foil, with ends of foil extending over sides. Mix wafer crumbs, ½ cup flour and brown sugar in medium bowl. Cut in margarine with pastry blender or 2 knives until mixture resembles coarse crumbs; press onto bottom of prepared pan. Bake 15 min.

2. **MEANWHILE,** beat Neufchâtel and granulated sugar with mixer until well blended. Add eggs and 2 Tbsp. flour; mix well. Blend in lemon zest, lemon juice and baking powder; pour over crust.

3. **BAKE** 25 to 28 min. or until center is set. Cool completely. Refrigerate 2 hours. Sprinkle with powdered sugar just before serving.

SPECIAL EXTRA:
Garnish with lemon peel.

pecan tassies

▸ what you need!

4 oz. (½ of 8-oz. pkg.) PHILADELPHIA Cream Cheese, softened

½ cup (1 stick) butter or margarine, softened

1 cup flour

1 egg

¾ cup packed brown sugar

1 tsp. vanilla

¾ cup finely chopped PLANTERS Pecans

3 squares BAKER'S Semi-Sweet Chocolate, melted

▸ make it!

1. **BEAT** cream cheese and butter in large bowl with mixer until well blended. Add flour; mix well. Refrigerate 1 hour or until chilled.

2. **HEAT** oven to 350°F. Divide dough into 24 balls; place 1 in each of 24 miniature muffin pan cups; press onto bottoms and up sides of cups to form shells. Beat egg in medium bowl. Add sugar and vanilla; mix well. Stir in nuts; spoon into pastry shells, filling each ¾ full.

3. **BAKE** 25 min. or until lightly browned. Let stand 5 min. in pans; remove to wire racks. Cool completely. Drizzle with melted chocolate. Let stand until set.

VARIATION:
For a quick garnish, dust cooled tarts with powdered sugar instead of drizzling with the melted chocolate.

HOW TO SOFTEN CREAM CHEESE:
Place measured amount of cream cheese in microwaveable bowl. Microwave on HIGH 10 sec. or until slightly softened.

PHILADELPHIA marble brownies

PREP: 20 min. | TOTAL: 1 hour | MAKES: 32 servings.

▶ what you need!

1 pkg. (19 to 21 oz.) brownie mix (13×9-inch pan size)

1 pkg. (8 oz.) PHILADELPHIA Cream Cheese, softened

⅓ cup sugar

1 egg

½ tsp. vanilla

½ cup BAKER'S Semi-Sweet Chocolate Chunks

▶ make it!

HEAT oven to 350°F.

1. **PREPARE** brownie batter as directed on package; spread into greased 13×9-inch pan.

2. **BEAT** cream cheese with mixer until creamy. Add sugar, egg and vanilla; mix well. Drop by tablespoonfuls over brownie batter; swirl with knife. Top with chocolate chunks.

3. **BAKE** 35 to 40 min. or until cream cheese mixture is lightly browned. Cool completely before cutting to serve. Keep refrigerated.

NOTE:
For best results, do not use brownie mix with a syrup pouch.

SUBSTITUTE:
Prepare using PHILADELPHIA Neufchâtel Cheese.

VARIATION:
Prepare as directed, omitting the chocolate chunks.

SPECIAL EXTRA:
After brownies have cooled, use a small round cookie cutter, about 1 inch in diameter, to cut small, delicate petit-four-type brownies.

double-layer pumpkin cheesecake

PREP: 10 min. | TOTAL: 4 hours 20 min. (incl. refrigerating) | MAKES: 8 servings.

▶ what you need!

2 pkg. (8 oz. each) PHILADELPHIA Fat Free Cream Cheese, softened

½ cup sugar

½ tsp. vanilla

2 eggs

½ cup canned pumpkin

¼ tsp. ground cinnamon

Dash ground nutmeg

⅓ cup HONEY MAID Graham Cracker Crumbs

½ cup thawed COOL WHIP Sugar Free Whipped Topping

▶ make it!

HEAT oven to 325°F.

1. **BEAT** cream cheese, sugar and vanilla with mixer until well blended. Beat in eggs, 1 at a time, just until blended. Remove 1 cup batter; place in medium bowl. Stir in pumpkin and spices.

2. **SPRAY** 9-inch pie plate with cooking spray; sprinkle bottom with crumbs.

3. **TOP** with layers of plain and pumpkin batters. Bake 40 min. or until center is almost set. Cool completely. Refrigerate 3 hours. Serve topped with COOL WHIP.

SPECIAL EXTRA:
Garnish with additional cinnamon.

NUTRITION BONUS:
Each serving of this creamy cheesecake is both rich in vitamin A from the pumpkin and an excellent source of calcium from the cream cheese.

freestyle apple tart

PREP: 15 min. | TOTAL: 40 min. | MAKES: 8 servings.

▶ what you need!

1 ready-to-use refrigerated pie crust (½ of 15-oz. pkg.)

4 oz. (½ of 8-oz. pkg.) PHILADELPHIA Cream Cheese, softened

3 red and/or green apples (1¼ lb.), thinly sliced

¼ cup granulated sugar

2 Tbsp. flour

1 tsp. cinnamon sugar

1 cup thawed COOL WHIP Whipped Topping

▶ make it!

HEAT oven to 450°F.

1. **LINE** 9-inch pie plate with crust. Carefully spread cream cheese into 6-inch circle in center.

2. **TOSS** apples with granulated sugar and flour; spoon over cream cheese.

3. **FOLD** crust partially over apples; sprinkle with cinnamon sugar. Bake 25 min., covering loosely with foil the last 5 min. Cool. Serve topped with COOL WHIP. Refrigerate leftovers.

VARIATION:
Prepare using PHILADELPHIA ⅓ Less Fat than Cream Cheese and COOL WHIP LITE Whipped Topping.

NOTE:
For best results, use baking apples for this recipe, such as Granny Smith, Golden Delicious and McIntosh.

SPECIAL EXTRA:
Stir additional ½ tsp. cinnamon sugar into the COOL WHIP before using as directed.

HOW TO MAKE CINNAMON SUGAR:
For each teaspoon of cinnamon sugar, mix ¾ tsp. granulated sugar and ¼ tsp. ground cinnamon.

PHILADELPHIA 3-STEP
key lime cheesecake

PREP: 10 min. plus refrigerating | MAKES: 8 servings.

▶ what you need!

2 pkg. (8 oz. each) PHILADELPHIA Cream Cheese, softened

½ cup sugar

1 tsp. lime zest

2 Tbsp. lime juice

½ tsp. vanilla

2 eggs

1 HONEY MAID Graham Pie Crust (6 oz.)

1 cup thawed COOL WHIP Whipped Topping

▶ make it!

HEAT oven to 350°F.

1. **BEAT** first 5 ingredients with mixer until well blended. Add eggs; mix just until blended.

2. **POUR** into crust.

3. **BAKE** 40 min. or until center is almost set. Cool. Refrigerate 3 hours. Top with COOL WHIP just before serving.

SIZE-WISE:
An occasional dessert can be part of a balanced diet, but remember to keep tabs on portions.

SPECIAL EXTRA:
Garnish with lime slices just before serving.

peanut butter cup pie

PREP: 15 min. plus refrigerating | MAKES: 10 servings.

▸ what you need!

1 pkg. (8 oz.) PHILADELPHIA Cream Cheese, softened

½ cup plus 1 Tbsp. creamy peanut butter, divided

1 cup cold milk

1 pkg. (3.4 oz.) JELL-O Vanilla Flavor Instant Pudding

2½ cups thawed COOL WHIP Whipped Topping, divided

1 OREO Pie Crust (6 oz.)

3 squares BAKER'S Semi-Sweet Chocolate

▸ make it!

1. **BEAT** cream cheese and ½ cup peanut butter until well blended. Add milk and dry pudding mix; beat 2 min. Whisk in 1 cup COOL WHIP; spoon into crust. Refrigerate until ready to use.

2. **MEANWHILE,** microwave remaining COOL WHIP and chocolate in microwaveable bowl on HIGH 1½ to 2 min. or until chocolate is completely melted and mixture is well blended, stirring after each minute. Cool completely.

3. **SPREAD** chocolate mixture over pudding layer in crust. Microwave remaining peanut butter in small microwaveable bowl 30 sec.; stir. Drizzle over pie. Refrigerate 4 hours or until firm.

HEALTHY LIVING:
Save 60 calories and 6 grams of fat, including 3 grams of saturated fat, per serving by preparing with PHILADELPHIA Neufchâtel Cheese, fat-free milk, JELL-O Vanilla Flavor Fat Free Sugar Free Instant Pudding and COOL WHIP LITE Whipped Topping.

SUBSTITUTE:
Prepare using JELL-O Chocolate Instant Pudding.

Make-Ahead Appetizers

Cold dips and nibbles that can be made in advance

cucumber roulades

PREP: 10 min. | MAKES: 6 servings.

▶ ## what you need!

1 seedless cucumber, peeled

¼ cup PHILADELPHIA Chive & Onion Cream Cheese Spread

1 oz. smoked salmon, thinly sliced, cut into 12 pieces

12 sprigs fresh dill

▶ ## make it!

1. **CUT** cucumber into 12 slices.

2. **USE** melon baller to scoop out indentation in center of each.

3. **FILL** with cream cheese spread; top with salmon and dill.

SUBSTITUTE:
Substitute 12 canned baby shrimp for the salmon.

PHILADELPHIA dessert dip

PREP: 5 min. | MAKES: 1¾ cups or 14 servings, 2 Tbsp. each.

▶ what you need!

1 pkg. (8 oz.) PHILADELPHIA Cream Cheese, softened

1 jar (7 oz.) JET-PUFFED Marshmallow Creme

▶ make it!

1. **MIX** ingredients until blended.

2. **SERVE** with assorted NABISCO Cookies or cut-up fresh fruit.

MAKE AHEAD:
Dip can be made ahead of time. Refrigerate until ready to serve.

SUBSTITUTE:
Prepare using PHILADELPHIA Neufchâtel Cheese.

MALLOW FRUIT DIP:
Prepare as directed, adding 1 Tbsp. orange juice, 1 tsp. orange zest and a dash of ground ginger.

HOW TO SOFTEN CREAM CHEESE:
Place completely unwrapped package of cream cheese on microwaveable plate. Microwave on HIGH 10 to 15 sec. or until slightly softened.

MAKE IT EASY:
To easily remove marshmallow creme from jar, remove lid and seal. Microwave on HIGH 30 sec. before removing marshmallow creme from jar.

sun-dried tomato & garlic dip

PREP: 5 min. | MAKES: 2 cups or 16 servings, 2 Tbsp. each.

▶ what you need!

1 tub (8 oz.) PHILADELPHIA Cream Cheese Spread

½ cup MIRACLE WHIP Dressing

½ cup sun-dried tomatoes packed in oil, drained, chopped

2 Tbsp. finely chopped fresh chives

1 clove garlic, minced

1 tsp. black pepper

▶ make it!

1. **MIX** all ingredients until well blended.

2. **SERVE** with cut-up fresh vegetables and NABISCO Crackers, if desired.

   MAKE AHEAD:
   This dip can be made up to 24 hours in advance. The longer you leave this dip in the refrigerator, the better the flavor.

mexican layered dip

▶ what you need!

1 pkg. (8 oz.) PHILADELPHIA Neufchâtel Cheese, softened

1 Tbsp. TACO BELL® HOME ORIGINALS® Taco Seasoning Mix

1 cup TACO BELL® HOME ORIGINALS® Thick 'N Chunky Salsa

1 cup rinsed canned black beans

1 cup shredded lettuce

1 cup KRAFT 2% Milk Shredded Cheddar Cheese

4 green onions, chopped

2 Tbsp. sliced black olives

▶ make it!

1. **BEAT** Neufchâtel with mixer until creamy. Add seasoning mix; mix well. Spread onto bottom of 9-inch pie plate or serving plate.

2. **TOP** with remaining ingredients.

3. **REFRIGERATE** 1 hour. Serve with assorted cut-up fresh vegetables.

SPECIAL EXTRA:
Garnish with chopped fresh cilantro.

PHILADELPHIA tuscan dip

PREP: 10 min. | REFRIGERATE: 1 hour | TOTAL: 1 hour 10 min. (incl. refrigerating) | MAKES: 1½ cups or 12 servings, 2 Tbsp. each.

▸ what you need!

1 pkg. (8 oz.) PHILADELPHIA Cream Cheese, softened

2 Tbsp. BREAKSTONE'S or KNUDSEN Sour Cream

½ cup finely chopped sun-dried tomatoes

½ cup chopped black olives

¼ cup finely chopped red onions

▸ make it!

1. **MIX** cream cheese and sour cream in medium bowl until well blended.

2. **ADD** remaining ingredients; mix well.

3. **REFRIGERATE** 1 hour. Serve with WHEAT THINS Crackers or cut-up fresh vegetables.

HEALTHY LIVING:
Save 30 calories and 3.5 grams of fat per serving by preparing with PHILADELPHIA Neufchâtel Cheese and BREAKSTONE'S Reduced Fat or KNUDSEN Light Sour Cream.

SUBSTITUTE:
Substitute kalamata olives for the black olives.

HOW TO HYDRATE SUN-DRIED TOMATOES:
Place tomatoes in small bowl; pour boiling water over tomatoes to cover. Let stand 5 to 10 min. to soften tomatoes. Drain; pat dry.

salsa roll-ups

PREP: 10 min. | MAKES: 10 servings.

▸ what you need!

4 oz. (½ of 8-oz. pkg.) PHILADELPHIA Neufchâtel Cheese, softened

3 Tbsp. TACO BELL® HOME ORIGINALS® Thick 'N Chunky Salsa

4 flour tortillas (6 inch)

½ cup KRAFT Mexican Style 2% Milk Finely Shredded Four Cheese

¼ tsp. chili powder

▸ make it!

1. **MIX** Neufchâtel and salsa; spread onto tortillas. Top with remaining ingredients.

2. **ROLL** up tortillas tightly. Cut each crosswise into 5 slices.

SPECIAL EXTRA:
Garnish with fresh cilantro.

PIZZA ROLL-UPS:
Prepare as directed, substituting pizza sauce for the salsa, KRAFT Shredded Italian* Mozzarella-Parmesan Cheese Blend for the Mexican style cheese and dried oregano leaves for the chili powder.

BLT ROLL-UPS:
Omit salsa, shredded cheese and chili powder. Spread tortillas with Neufchâtel as directed. Top with 1 cup shredded lettuce, 2 Tbsp. OSCAR MAYER Bacon Pieces and 1 chopped tomato. Roll up and slice as directed.

MAKE AHEAD:
Prepare roll-ups as directed, but do not cut into slices. Tightly wrap each roll-up in plastic wrap. Refrigerate up to 4 hours. Slice just before serving.

* Made with quality cheeses crafted in the USA.

TACO BELL® and HOME ORIGINALS® are trademarks owned and licensed by Taco Bell Corp.

flavor-infused cream cheese nibbles

PREP: 10 min. plus refrigerating | MAKES: 18 servings, 2 pieces each.

▶ what you need!

1 pkg. (8 oz.) PHILADELPHIA Cream Cheese

½ cup KRAFT Sun-Dried Tomato Dressing

2 cloves garlic, sliced

3 small sprigs fresh rosemary, stems removed

6 sprigs fresh thyme, chopped

1 tsp. black peppercorns

Peel of 1 lemon, cut into thin strips

▶ make it!

1. **CUT** cream cheese into 36 pieces; place in shallow dish.

2. **ADD** remaining ingredients; mix lightly.

3. **REFRIGERATE** 1 hour. Serve with NABISCO Crackers, crusty bread or pita chips.

CREATIVE LEFTOVERS:
Let the cheese come to room temperature before serving.

SHORTCUT:
To simplify, spread softened cream cheese onto bottom of 9-inch pie plate instead of cutting into pieces. Chop garlic, rosemary, thyme and lemon peel. Mix with dressing and ¼ tsp. ground black pepper; spread over cream cheese. Serve as directed.

MAKE AHEAD:
Appetizer can be stored in refrigerator up to 24 hours before serving.

PHILLY shrimp cocktail dip

PREP: 10 min. | MAKES: 3 cups or 24 servings, 2 Tbsp. each.

▸ what you need!

1 pkg. (8 oz.) PHILADELPHIA Cream Cheese, softened

¾ lb. cooked cleaned shrimp, chopped (about 2 cups)

¾ cup KRAFT Cocktail Sauce

¼ cup KRAFT Shredded Parmesan Cheese

2 green onions, sliced

▸ make it!

1. **SPREAD** cream cheese onto bottom of shallow bowl.

2. **TOSS** shrimp with cocktail sauce; spoon over cream cheese.

3. **TOP** with remaining ingredients. Serve with WHEAT THINS Original Crackers.

SUBSTITUTE:
Substitute 1 pkg. (8 oz.) imitation crabmeat, coarsely chopped, for the shrimp.

pesto crostini

▶ what you need!

3 cups fresh basil leaves

⅓ cup KRAFT Classic Italian Vinaigrette Dressing

⅓ cup KRAFT Grated Parmesan Cheese

32 baguette slices (¼-inch thick), toasted

1 tub (8 oz.) PHILADELPHIA Cream Cheese Spread

¼ cup KRAFT Grated Parmesan Cheese

▶ make it!

1. **BLEND** basil, dressing and ⅓ cup Parmesan in blender until smooth.

2. **SPREAD** toast slices with cream cheese spread, then basil mixture.

3. **SPRINKLE** with remaining Parmesan.

STORAGE KNOW-HOW:
Wrap stems of basil in a damp paper towel, place in resealable plastic bag and refrigerate up to 4 days. Or place the bunch, stem ends down, in a glass of water; cover with a plastic bag and refrigerate as directed.

SPECIAL EXTRA:
To make a black olive pesto, prepare as directed adding ½ cup pitted black olives to the blender with the basil.

Visual Aha!
Show on a white
square-shaped
platter.

creamy crab and red pepper spread

PREP: 15 min. plus refrigerating | **MAKES:** 2¼ cups or 18 servings, 2 Tbsp. cheese spread and 5 crackers each.

▸ what you need!

2 green onions, thinly sliced, divided

1 tub (8 oz.) PHILADELPHIA ⅓ Less Fat than Cream Cheese

1 can (6 oz.) lump crabmeat, drained

½ cup KRAFT 2% Milk Shredded Sharp Cheddar Cheese

½ cup finely chopped red bell peppers

1 Tbsp. GREY POUPON Dijon Mustard

RITZ Reduced Fat Crackers

▸ make it!

1. **REMOVE** 2 Tbsp. onions; set aside. Mix remaining onions with all remaining ingredients except crackers.

2. **REFRIGERATE** 1 hour.

3. **SPRINKLE** with reserved onions. Serve with crackers.

NUTRITION BONUS:
The red peppers provide flavor, color and a good source of vitamin C in this cheesy spread.

PHILADELPHIA creamy salsa dip

PREP: 5 min. | **TOTAL: 5 min.** | **MAKES: 2 cups or 16 servings, 2 Tbsp. each.**

▶ what you need!

1 pkg. (8 oz.) PHILADELPHIA Cream Cheese, softened

1 cup TACO BELL® HOME ORIGINALS® Thick 'N Chunky Salsa

▶ make it!

1. **MIX** ingredients until well blended.

2. **SERVE** with assorted cut-up fresh vegetables or tortilla chips.

SPECIAL EXTRA:
Top prepared dip with layers of 1 rinsed can (15 oz.) black beans and 1 cup of your favorite variety of KRAFT Mexican Style Finely Shredded Cheese.

PHILADELPHIA CREAMY BACON-RANCH DIP:
Prepare dip as directed, substituting ½ cup KRAFT Ranch Dressing for the salsa and stirring in ¼ cup OSCAR MAYER Real Bacon Bits with the dressing.

SUBSTITUTE:
Prepare using PHILADELPHIA Neufchâtel Cheese.

MAKE AHEAD:
Dip can be made ahead of time. Store in refrigerator until ready to serve.

MAKE YOUR OWN BAKED TORTILLA CHIPS:
Cut flour tortillas into desired shapes. Place in single layer on baking sheet. Bake at 350°F for 8 to 10 min. or until crisp. Cool on wire racks.

TACO BELL® and HOME ORIGINALS® are trademarks owned and licensed by Taco Bell Corp.

PHILLY mediterranean dip

PREP: 10 min. | MAKES: 1½ cups or 12 servings, 2 Tbsp. each.

▸ what you need!

1 pkg. (8 oz.) PHILADELPHIA Neufchâtel Cheese, softened

½ cup chopped seedless cucumbers

1 plum tomato, chopped

2 Tbsp. finely chopped red onions

2 Tbsp. KRAFT Greek Vinaigrette Dressing

▸ make it!

1. **SPREAD** Neufchâtel onto bottom of 9-inch pie plate.

2. **COMBINE** remaining ingredients; spoon over Neufchâtel.

3. **SERVE** with WHEAT THINS Original Crackers or assorted cut-up fresh vegetables.

HOW TO SOFTEN NEUFCHÂTEL CHEESE:
Place completely unwrapped Neufchâtel in microwaveable 9-inch pie plate. Microwave on HIGH 15 sec. or just until softened. Spread onto bottom of pie plate, then continue as directed.

spring veggie pizza appetizer

PREP: 20 min. | TOTAL: 2 hours 35 min. (incl. refrigerating) | MAKES: 32 servings.

▶ what you need!

2 pkg. (8 oz. each) refrigerated crescent dinner rolls

1 tub (8 oz.) PHILADELPHIA Cream Cheese Spread

½ cup MIRACLE WHIP Dressing

1 tsp. dill weed

½ tsp. onion salt

1 cup each chopped sugar snap peas and quartered cherry tomatoes

½ cup each sliced radishes, chopped yellow bell peppers and shredded carrots

▶ make it!

HEAT oven to 375°F.

1. **UNROLL** dough; separate into 4 rectangles. Press onto bottom and up sides of 15×10×1-inch pan, firmly pressing seams and perforations together to seal.

2. **BAKE** 11 to 13 min. or until golden brown; cool.

3. **MIX** cream cheese spread, dressing, dill weed and onion salt until well blended; spread onto crust. Top with remaining ingredients. Refrigerate 2 hours.

SUBSTITUTE:
Substitute chopped cucumbers and/or chopped red bell peppers for any of the chopped vegetables.

NUTRITION BONUS:
The veggies in these colorful appetizers team up to provide a good source of vitamin C.

favorite topped deviled eggs

PREP: 15 min. | MAKES: 24 servings.

▶ what you need!

12 hard-cooked eggs

4 oz. (½ of 8-oz. pkg.) PHILADELPHIA Neufchâtel Cheese, softened

3 Tbsp. KRAFT Light Mayo Reduced Fat Mayonnaise

2 tsp. GREY POUPON Dijon Mustard

2 tsp. white vinegar

1 tsp. sugar

⅛ tsp. paprika

▶ make it!

1. **CUT** eggs lengthwise in half. Remove yolks; place in medium bowl. Add all remaining ingredients except paprika; mix well.

2. **SPOON** into resealable plastic bag. Cut small corner from bottom of bag; pipe filling into egg whites. Sprinkle with paprika.

3. **ADD** Toppings, if desired.

TOPPING VARIATIONS:
Country Favorite: Top with 10 slices cooked and crumbled OSCAR MAYER Bacon and 2 finely chopped green onions.
It's Italian: Top with ½ cup thinly sliced drained jarred sun-dried tomatoes packed in oil and ¼ cup thinly sliced fresh basil. **Fiesta Time:** Top with 6 Tbsp. finely chopped red peppers and 1 Tbsp. chopped cilantro. **Coastal Delight:** Top with ½ cup drained canned baby shrimp and 2 Tbsp. chopped fresh dill.

MAKE AHEAD:
Prepare as directed. Store in tightly covered container in refrigerator until ready to serve.

turkey peppercorn ranch bites

PREP: 15 min. | MAKES: 12 servings.

▶ what you need!

2 oz. (¼ of 8-oz. pkg.) PHILADELPHIA Neufchâtel Cheese, softened

¼ cup KRAFT FREE Peppercorn Ranch Dressing

3 flour tortillas (6 inch)

1 pkg. (6 oz.) OSCAR MAYER Thin Sliced Oven Roasted Turkey Breast

12 CLAUSSEN Bread 'N Butter Pickle Chips

▶ make it!

1. **MIX** Neufchâtel and dressing until well blended.

2. **SPREAD** onto tortillas; top with turkey. Roll up tightly.

3. **CUT** each roll-up into 4 slices. Top with pickles; secure with wooden picks.

VARIATION:
To serve warm, prepare as directed; place on microwaveable plate. Microwave on HIGH 1 min. or just until warmed.

SPECIAL EXTRA:
Sprinkle ½ cup shredded lettuce over each topped tortilla before rolling up.

NUTRITION BONUS:
Help your friends and family eat right with these tasty low-fat appetizers.

Hot & Savory Appetizers

Warm and cheesy dips and small bites

baked crab rangoon

PREP: 20 min. | TOTAL: 40 min. | MAKES: 12 servings.

▶ what you need!

4 oz. (½ of 8-oz. pkg.) PHILADELPHIA Neufchâtel Cheese, softened

1 can (6 oz.) crabmeat, drained, flaked

2 green onions, thinly sliced

¼ cup KRAFT Light Mayo Reduced Fat Mayonnaise

12 wonton wrappers

▶ make it!

HEAT oven to 350°F.

1. **MIX** first 4 ingredients.

2. **PLACE** 1 wonton wrapper in each of 12 muffin cups sprayed with cooking spray, extending edges of wrappers over sides of cups. Fill with crab mixture.

3. **BAKE** 18 to 20 min. or until edges of cups are golden brown and filling is heated through.

SPECIAL EXTRA:
Garnish with additional green onions, cut into strips, just before serving.

savory parmesan bites

PREP: 15 min. | TOTAL: 30 min. | MAKES: 32 servings.

▸ what you need!

1 pkg. (8 oz.) PHILADELPHIA Cream Cheese, softened

1 cup KRAFT Grated Parmesan Cheese, divided

2 cans (8 oz. each) refrigerated crescent dinner rolls

1 red pepper, chopped

¼ cup chopped fresh parsley

▸ make it!

HEAT oven to 350°F.

1. **BEAT** cream cheese and ¾ cup Parmesan with mixer until well blended.

2. **SEPARATE** dough into 8 rectangles; seal seams. Spread with cream cheese mixture; top with peppers and parsley. Fold each rectangle lengthwise into thirds to enclose filling; cut each into 4 squares. Place, seam-sides down, on baking sheet; top with remaining Parmesan.

3. **BAKE** 13 to 15 min. or until golden brown.

SIZE-WISE:
At your next party, select a few of your favorite appetizers rather than sampling one of each to save room for your entrée.

VARIATION:
Substitute 1 jar (13¼ oz.) sliced mushrooms or 1 pkg. (3 oz.) pepperoni slices for the red peppers and parsley.

cream cheese-bacon crescents

PREP: 15 min. | TOTAL: 30 min. | MAKES: 16 servings.

▶ what you need!

1 tub (8 oz.) PHILADELPHIA Chive & Onion Cream Cheese Spread

3 slices OSCAR MAYER Bacon, cooked, crumbled

2 cans (8 oz. each) refrigerated crescent dinner rolls

▶ make it!

HEAT oven to 375°F.

1. **MIX** cream cheese spread and bacon until well blended.

2. **SEPARATE** each can of dough into 8 triangles. Cut each triangle lengthwise in half. Spread each dough triangle with 1 generous tsp. cream cheese mixture. Roll up, starting at shortest side of triangle; place, point sides down, on baking sheet.

3. **BAKE** 12 to 15 min. or until golden brown. Serve warm.

HEALTHY LIVING:
For a reduced-fat version, prepare using PHILADELPHIA Chive & Onion Light Cream Cheese Spread and reduced-fat refrigerated crescent dinner rolls. As a bonus, these changes will save 30 calories per serving.

VARIATION:
For a sweet version, prepare using PHILADELPHIA Strawberry Cream Cheese Spread and substituting chopped PLANTERS Walnuts for the bacon.

make-ahead spinach phyllo roll-ups

PREP: 30 min. | TOTAL: 55 min. | MAKES: 30 servings or 5 logs, 6 servings each.

▶ what you need!

- 1 egg, beaten
- 1 pkg. (10 oz.) frozen chopped spinach, thawed, drained
- 1 cup ATHENOS Traditional Crumbled Feta Cheese
- 1 tub (8 oz.) PHILADELPHIA ⅓ Less Fat than Cream Cheese with Garden Vegetables
- 4 green onions, finely chopped
- 15 sheets frozen phyllo (14×9 inch), thawed
- ⅓ cup butter, melted

▶ make it!

1. **MIX** first 5 ingredients until well blended; set aside. Brush 1 phyllo sheet lightly with butter; top with 2 more phyllo sheets, lightly brushing each layer with some of the remaining butter. Place remaining phyllo between sheets of plastic wrap; set aside.

2. **SPREAD** ⅕ of the spinach mixture along 1 short side of phyllo stack; fold in both long sides then roll up, starting at 1 of the short sides to make log. Repeat with remaining phyllo sheets and spinach mixture to make 4 more logs. Brush with remaining butter. Make small cuts in tops of logs at 1-inch intervals. Place in large freezer-weight resealable plastic bags or wrap tightly in plastic wrap.

3. **FREEZE** up to 3 months. When ready to bake, remove desired number of logs from freezer. Refrigerate, tightly wrapped, several hours or overnight until thawed. Unwrap, then place on baking sheet. Bake in 375°F oven 25 min. or until golden brown. Cool on baking sheet 5 min.; transfer to cutting board. Use serrated knife to cut each log into 6 slices.

SPECIAL EXTRA:
Garnish with cilantro and lime wedges.

cheesy spinach and bacon dip

PREP: 10 min. | TOTAL: 15 min. | MAKES: 4 cups or 32 servings, 2 Tbsp. each.

▶ what you need!

1 pkg. (10 oz.) frozen chopped spinach, thawed, drained

1 lb. (16 oz.) VELVEETA Pasteurized Prepared Cheese Product, cut into ½-inch cubes

4 oz. (½ of 8-oz. pkg.) PHILADELPHIA Cream Cheese, cubed

1 can (10 oz.) RO*TEL Diced Tomatoes & Green Chilies, undrained

8 slices OSCAR MAYER Bacon, cooked, crumbled

▶ make it!

1. **MICROWAVE** ingredients in microwaveable bowl on HIGH 5 min. or until VELVEETA is completely melted and mixture is well blended, stirring after 3 min.

2. **SERVE** with WHEAT THINS Crackers and cut-up fresh vegetables.

VARIATION:
Prepare using VELVEETA 2% Milk Pasteurized Prepared Cheese Product and PHILADELPHIA Neufchâtel Cheese.

TO HALVE:
Cut ingredients in half; combine in microwaveable bowl. Microwave on HIGH 3 to 4 min. or until VELVEETA is completely melted and mixture is well blended, stirring after 2 min. Serve as directed. Makes 2 cups or 16 servings, 2 Tbsp. each.

KEEPING IT SAFE:
Hot dips should be discarded after sitting at room temperature for 2 hours or longer.

HOW TO CUT UP VELVEETA:
Cut VELVEETA (the whole loaf) into ½-inch-thick slices. Then, cut each slice crosswise in both directions to make cubes.

CREATIVE LEFTOVERS:
Refrigerate any leftover dip. Then, reheat and toss with your favorite hot cooked pasta.

USE YOUR SLOW COOKER:
When serving this dip at a party, pour the prepared dip into a small slow cooker set on LOW. This will keep the dip warm and at the ideal consistency for several hours. For best results, stir the dip occasionally to prevent hot spots.

Ro*Tel is a product of ConAgra Foods, Inc.

baked triple-veggie dip

PREP: 15 min. | TOTAL: 50 min. | MAKES: 4½ cups or 36 servings, 2 Tbsp. each.

▶ what you need!

1½ cups KRAFT Grated Parmesan Cheese, divided

1 can (1 lb. 3 oz.) asparagus spears, drained, chopped

1 pkg. (10 oz.) frozen chopped spinach, thawed, drained

1 can (8½ oz.) artichoke hearts, drained, chopped

1 tub (8 oz.) PHILADELPHIA Chive & Onion Cream Cheese Spread

½ cup KRAFT Real Mayo Mayonnaise

▶ make it!

HEAT oven to 375°F.

1. **MIX** 1¼ cups Parmesan with all remaining ingredients.

2. **SPOON** into 2-qt. baking dish; top with remaining Parmesan.

3. **BAKE** 35 min. or until dip is heated through and top is lightly browned.

VARIATION:
Prepare as directed, using KRAFT Reduced Fat Parmesan Style Grated Topping, PHILADELPHIA Chive & Onion ⅓ Less Fat than Cream Cheese and KRAFT Mayo with Olive Oil Reduced Fat Mayonnaise.

NUTRITION BONUS:
The spinach is a good source of vitamin A in this tasty baked dip.

mini florentine cups

PREP: 20 min. | TOTAL: 35 min. | MAKES: 24 servings.

▶ what you need!

1 pkg. (10 oz.) frozen chopped spinach, cooked, well drained

½ cup KRAFT 2% Milk Shredded Mozzarella Cheese

⅓ cup PHILADELPHIA ⅓ Less Fat than Cream Cheese

1 Tbsp. KRAFT Grated Parmesan Cheese

1 Tbsp. finely chopped onions

¼ tsp. garlic powder

24 slices OSCAR MAYER Deli Fresh Shaved Oven Roasted Turkey Breast

▶ make it!

HEAT oven to 350°F.

1. **COMBINE** all ingredients except turkey.

2. **FLATTEN** turkey slices; place 1 slice on bottom and up side of each of 24 miniature muffin cups. Fill with spinach mixture.

3. **BAKE** 15 min. or until heated through. Cool in pan 5 min. before removing from pan to serve.

MAKE AHEAD:
Having a party? Assemble appetizers several hours in advance. Refrigerate until ready to serve. Then, uncover and bake as directed.

SPECIAL EXTRA:
Add 1 to 2 Tbsp. chopped water chestnuts to the spinach mixture before spooning into prepared cups.

SUBSTITUTE:
Prepare using OSCAR MAYER Deli Fresh Shaved Smoked Ham.

NUTRITION BONUS:
These tasty low-fat appetizers are great for entertaining. As a bonus, they're rich in vitamin A from the spinach.

cheesy hot crab and red pepper spread

PREP: 10 min. | TOTAL: 30 min. | MAKES: 3 cups spread or 24 servings, 2 Tbsp. spread and 16 crackers each.

▶ what you need!

1 pkg. (8 oz.) PHILADELPHIA Neufchâtel Cheese, softened

1½ cups KRAFT 2% Milk Shredded Mozzarella Cheese

1 tsp. garlic powder

1 tsp. Italian seasoning

1 red pepper, chopped

1 small onion, finely chopped

1 can (6 oz.) crabmeat, drained

WHEAT THINS Original Crackers

▶ make it!

HEAT oven to 375°F.

1. **MIX** all ingredients except crackers until well blended.

2. **SPREAD** into 9-inch pie plate.

3. **BAKE** 20 min. or until crab mixture is heated through and top is lightly browned. Serve with crackers.

MAKE AHEAD:
Prepare spread as directed, but do not bake. Refrigerate up to 2 days. When ready to serve, bake at 375°F for 25 min. or until heated through. Serve as directed.

five-layer italian dip

PREP: 10 min. | TOTAL: 25 min. | MAKES: 2 cups or 16 servings, 2 Tbsp. each.

▶ what you need!

1 pkg. (8 oz.) PHILADELPHIA Cream Cheese, softened

¼ cup KRAFT Grated Parmesan Cheese

⅓ cup pesto

½ cup roasted red peppers, drained, chopped

1 cup KRAFT Shredded Mozzarella Cheese

▶ make it!

HEAT oven to 350°F.

1. **MIX** cream cheese and Parmesan; spread onto bottom of 9-inch pie plate.

2. **LAYER** remaining ingredients over cream cheese mixture.

3. **BAKE** 15 min. or until heated through. Serve with assorted NABISCO Crackers or sliced Italian bread.

VARIATION:
Prepare using PHILADELPHIA Neufchâtel Cheese and KRAFT 2% Milk Shredded Mozzarella Cheese.

SPECIAL EXTRA:
Garnish with sliced black olives and fresh basil leaves just before serving.

cheese & bacon jalapeño rellenos

PREP: 20 min. | TOTAL: 30 min. | MAKES: 18 servings.

▸ what you need!

4 oz. (½ of 8-oz. pkg.) PHILADELPHIA Cream Cheese, softened

1 cup KRAFT Shredded Cheddar Cheese

4 slices OSCAR MAYER Bacon, cooked, crumbled

2 Tbsp. finely chopped onions

2 Tbsp. chopped cilantro

1 clove garlic, minced

18 jalapeño peppers, cut lengthwise in half, seeds and membranes removed

▸ make it!

HEAT oven to 375°F.

1. **COMBINE** all ingredients except peppers; spoon into peppers.

2. **PLACE,** filled-sides up, on baking sheet.

3. **BAKE** 10 min. or until cheese is melted.

SUBSTITUTE:
Substitute 3 large red, yellow or green bell peppers, each cut into 6 triangles, for the jalapeño pepper halves. Top with cheese mixture before baking as directed.

SPECIAL EXTRA:
Add ¼ tsp. ground red pepper (cayenne) to the cream cheese mixture before spooning into peppers.

SUBSTITUTE:
Prepare using KRAFT Shredded Monterey Jack Cheese.

HOW TO HANDLE FRESH CHILE PEPPERS:
When handling fresh chile peppers, be sure to wear disposable rubber or clear plastic gloves to avoid irritating your skin. Never touch your eyes, nose or mouth when handling the peppers. If you've forgotten to wear the gloves and feel a burning sensation in your hands, apply a baking soda and water paste to the affected area. After rinsing the paste off, you should feel some relief.

easy-bake cheese & pesto

PREP: 10 min. | TOTAL: 40 min. | MAKES: 12 servings.

▸ what you need!

1 can (4 oz.) reduced-fat refrigerated crescent dinner rolls

1 pkg. (8 oz.) PHILADELPHIA Neufchâtel Cheese

2 Tbsp. pesto

2 Tbsp. chopped roasted red peppers

1 egg, beaten

▸ make it!

HEAT oven to 350°F.

1. **UNROLL** dough on lightly greased baking sheet; firmly press seams together to form 12×4-inch rectangle.

2. **CUT** Neufchâtel horizontally in half. Place 1 Neufchâtel piece on half of dough; top with 1 Tbsp. pesto and peppers. Cover with remaining Neufchâtel piece; spread with remaining pesto. Brush dough with egg; fold in half to enclose filling. Press edges of dough together to seal. Brush top with any remaining egg.

3. **BAKE** 15 to 18 min. or until lightly browned. Cool 10 min. Serve with RITZ Reduced Fat Crackers or cut-up fresh vegetables.

MAKE AHEAD:
Assemble recipe on baking sheet as directed. Refrigerate up to 4 hours. When ready to serve, uncover and bake as directed.

NUTRITION BONUS:
This tasty appetizer, made with better-for-you ingredients, can fit into a healthful eating plan.

heavenly ham roll-ups

PREP: 15 min. | TOTAL: 35 min. | MAKES: 15 servings.

▶ what you need!

1 pkg. (9 oz.) OSCAR MAYER Deli Fresh Shaved Smoked Ham

5 Tbsp. PHILADELPHIA ⅓ Less Fat than Cream Cheese

15 fresh asparagus spears (about 1 lb.), trimmed

▶ make it!

HEAT oven to 350°F.

1. **FLATTEN** ham slices; pat dry. Stack in piles of 2 slices each; spread each stack with 1 tsp. reduced-fat cream cheese.

2. **PLACE** 1 asparagus spear on 1 long side of each ham stack; roll up. Place, seam-sides down, in 13×9-inch baking dish.

3. **BAKE** 15 to 20 min. or until heated through.

NO-BAKE HEAVENLY HAM ROLL-UPS:
Substitute frozen asparagus spears, cooked as directed on package, or canned asparagus spears, heated if desired, for the fresh asparagus. Assemble roll-ups as directed. Serve immediately. Or, cover and refrigerate until ready to serve.

FOOD FACTS:
Asparagus spears should be a bright green color and free of blemishes. Choose stalks that are straight, uniformly sized (either all thick or all thin) and firm. Stand fresh asparagus spears upright in a container filled with an inch of water. Cover with a plastic bag and refrigerate up to 3 days.

MAKE AHEAD:
Assemble roll-ups as directed. Refrigerate up to 24 hours before baking as directed.

SUBSTITUTE:
Prepare as directed, using 1 pkg. (6 oz.) OSCAR MAYER Thin Sliced Smoked Ham. Substitute 1 slice of ham for every 2 slices of the shaved ham.

mini cream cheese and pepper jelly phyllo cups

PREP: 20 min. | TOTAL: 40 min. | MAKES: 3 doz. or 12 servings, 3 phyllo cups each.

▸ what you need!

6 frozen phyllo sheets, thawed

2 Tbsp. butter, melted

1 pkg. (8 oz.) PHILADELPHIA Cream Cheese, cut into 36 cubes

6 Tbsp. hot pepper jelly

▸ make it!

HEAT oven 350°F.

1. **BRUSH** 1 phyllo sheet with butter; top with second phyllo sheet. Brush with butter; cut into 24 (2-inch) squares. Stack 2 squares, on an angle, to make 4 thicknesses; repeat with remaining phyllo sheets and butter. Press 1 stack into each of 36 miniature (1½-inch) muffin cups.

2. **ADD** 1 cream cheese cube to each cup. Bake 20 min. or until cream cheese is melted and pastry is golden brown.

3. **TOP** each serving with ½ tsp. hot pepper jelly.

SIZE-WISE:
Select a few of your favorite appetizers rather than sampling one of each to save room for your entrée.

STORAGE KNOW-HOW:
Leftover phyllo sheets can be wrapped tightly and refrozen until ready to use.

MAKE IT EASY:
Prepare using purchased jalapeño jelly.

Pasta & Casseroles

Hearty one-dish meals

shrimp-in-love pasta

PREP: 10 min. | **TOTAL: 25 min.** | **MAKES: 2 servings.**

▶ what you need!

¼ lb. linguine, uncooked

1 cup uncooked deveined peeled medium shrimp

2 tomatoes, chopped

½ cup (½ of 8-oz. tub) PHILADELPHIA Cream Cheese Spread

1½ cups torn fresh spinach

▶ make it!

1. **COOK** linguine as directed on package.

2. **MEANWHILE,** heat large skillet on medium-high heat. Add shrimp, tomatoes and cream cheese spread; cook and stir 3 to 4 min. or until shrimp are done and mixture is well blended.

3. **DRAIN** linguine; place in large bowl. Add spinach; mix lightly. Stir in shrimp mixture.

   SUBSTITUTE:
   Prepare using 4 oz. (½ of 8-oz. pkg.) PHILADELPHIA Neufchâtel Cheese.

   TO DOUBLE:
   For 4 servings, prepare as directed using 1 tub (8 oz.) PHILADELPHIA Cream Cheese Spread and doubling all other ingredients.

creamy pasta primavera

▶ what you need!

3 cups penne pasta, uncooked

2 Tbsp. KRAFT Light Zesty Italian Dressing

1½ lb. boneless skinless chicken breasts, cut into 1-inch pieces

2 zucchini, cut into bite-size pieces

1½ cups cut-up fresh asparagus (1-inch lengths)

1 red pepper, chopped

1 cup fat-free reduced-sodium chicken broth

4 oz. (½ of 8-oz. pkg.) PHILADELPHIA Neufchâtel Cheese, cubed

¼ cup KRAFT Grated Parmesan Cheese

▶ make it!

1. **COOK** penne in large saucepan as directed on package.

2. **MEANWHILE,** heat dressing in large skillet on medium heat. Add chicken and vegetables; cook 10 to 12 min. or until chicken is done, stirring frequently. Add broth and Neufchâtel; cook 1 min. or until Neufchâtel is melted, stirring constantly. Stir in Parmesan.

3. **DRAIN** penne; return to pan. Add chicken mixture; toss lightly. Cook 1 min. or until heated through. (Sauce will thicken upon standing.)

NUTRITION BONUS:
Delight your loved ones with this creamy, yet low-calorie and low-fat, meal that is an easy way to add vegetables to your family's diet.

HOW TO MAKE IT MEATLESS:
Omit chicken. Prepare as directed, cooking vegetables until crisp-tender.

spaghetti with zesty bolognese

PREP: 10 min. | TOTAL: 30 min. | MAKES: 6 servings.

▶ what you need!

1 small onion, chopped

¼ cup KRAFT Light Zesty Italian Dressing

1 lb. extra-lean ground beef

1 can (15 oz.) tomato sauce

1 can (14 oz.) diced tomatoes, undrained

¾ lb. spaghetti, uncooked

2 Tbsp. PHILADELPHIA ⅓ Less Fat than Cream Cheese

¼ cup KRAFT Grated Parmesan Cheese

▶ make it!

1. **COOK** and stir onions in dressing in large skillet on medium heat until crisp-tender. Add meat; cook on medium-high heat until browned, stirring frequently. Stir in tomato sauce and tomatoes. Bring to boil; simmer on medium-low 15 min., stirring occasionally.

2. **MEANWHILE,** cook spaghetti as directed on package.

3. **REMOVE** sauce from heat. Add reduced-fat cream cheese; stir until melted. Drain spaghetti; place in large bowl. Top with sauce and Parmesan.

SUBSTITUTE:
Prepare using whole wheat or multi-grain spaghetti.

NUTRITION BONUS:
Everybody loves spaghetti! Feel good serving up this low-calorie, low-fat version of a family favorite.

creamy tomato
and chicken spaghetti

PREP: 10 min. | TOTAL: 25 min. | MAKES: 4 servings, about 2 cups each.

▶ what you need!

½ lb. spaghetti, uncooked

2 cups frozen stir-fry vegetables

1 Tbsp. oil

1 lb. boneless skinless chicken breasts, cut into strips

1 can (14.5 oz.) diced tomatoes, undrained

¼ cup KRAFT Zesty Italian Dressing

½ cup (½ of 8-oz. tub) PHILADELPHIA Cream Cheese Spread

¼ cup KRAFT Grated Parmesan Cheese

▶ make it!

1. **COOK** spaghetti in large saucepan as directed on package, adding stir-fry vegetables to the boiling water the last 3 min.

2. **MEANWHILE,** heat oil in large nonstick skillet on medium-high heat. Add chicken; cook 6 min., stirring occasionally. Stir in tomatoes and dressing; bring to boil. Simmer on medium heat 4 min., stirring occasionally. Add cream cheese spread; cook and stir until cream cheese is completely melted and mixture is well blended.

3. **DRAIN** spaghetti mixture; place in large bowl. Add chicken mixture; toss to coat. Sprinkle with Parmesan.

SUBSTITUTE:
Substitute your favorite frozen vegetables for the stir-fry vegetables. Or, use cut-up fresh vegetables; just add to the cooking water for the last 4 min. of the spaghetti cooking time.

quick pasta carbonara

▶ what you need!

½ lb. fettuccine, uncooked

4 slices OSCAR MAYER Bacon, chopped

4 oz. (½ of 8-oz. pkg.) PHILADELPHIA Cream Cheese, cubed

1 cup frozen peas

¾ cup milk

½ cup KRAFT Grated Parmesan Cheese

½ tsp. garlic powder

▶ make it!

1. **COOK** fettuccine as directed on package. Meanwhile, cook bacon in large skillet until crisp. Remove bacon from skillet with slotted spoon, reserving 2 Tbsp. drippings in skillet. Drain bacon on paper towels.

2. **ADD** remaining ingredients to reserved drippings; cook on low heat until cream cheese is melted and mixture is well blended and heated through.

3. **DRAIN** fettuccine; place in large bowl. Add cream cheese sauce and bacon; mix lightly.

KEEPING IT SAFE:
When a dish contains dairy products, such as the cheeses and milk in this recipe, be sure to serve it immediately and refrigerate any leftovers promptly.

SUBSTITUTE:
Prepare using PHILADELPHIA Neufchâtel Cheese.

SERVING SUGGESTION:
For added color and texture, serve with a mixed green salad tossed with your favorite KRAFT Light Dressing.

south-of-the-border chicken & pasta skillet

PREP: 10 min. | TOTAL: 35 min. | MAKES: 4 servings, 2 cups each.

▶ what you need!

2 cups medium-size pasta, uncooked

1 lb. boneless skinless chicken breasts, cut into bite-size pieces

1 jar (16 oz.) TACO BELL® HOME ORIGINALS® Thick 'N Chunky Salsa

1 pkg. (10 oz.) frozen corn

4 oz. (½ of 8-oz. pkg.) PHILADELPHIA Cream Cheese, cubed

¼ tsp. ground cumin

1 cup KRAFT Mexican Style Finely Shredded Four Cheese, divided

▶ make it!

1. **COOK** pasta as directed on package.

2. **MEANWHILE,** cook and stir chicken in large nonstick skillet sprayed with cooking spray on medium-high heat 6 min. or until done. Add salsa, corn, cream cheese and cumin; simmer on medium-low heat 6 min. or until cream cheese is melted, stirring occasionally.

3. **DRAIN** pasta; add to skillet with ½ cup shredded cheese. Stir; simmer 3 min. or until heated through. Top with remaining shredded cheese; cover. Remove from heat. Let stand until melted.

SPECIAL EXTRA:
Sprinkle with chopped cilantro before serving.

TACO BELL® and HOME ORIGINALS® are trademarks owned and licensed by Taco Bell Corp.

three-cheese chicken penne pasta bake

PREP: 20 min. | TOTAL: 43 min. | MAKES: 4 servings.

▶ what you need!

1½ cups multi-grain penne pasta, uncooked

1 pkg. (9 oz.) fresh spinach leaves

1 lb. boneless skinless chicken breasts, cut into bite-size pieces

1 tsp. dried basil leaves

1 jar (14½ oz.) spaghetti sauce

1 can (14½ oz.) diced tomatoes, drained

2 oz. (¼ of 8-oz. pkg.) PHILADELPHIA Neufchâtel Cheese, cubed

1 cup KRAFT 2% Milk Shredded Mozzarella Cheese, divided

2 Tbsp. KRAFT Grated Parmesan Cheese

▶ make it!

HEAT oven to 375°F.

1. **COOK** pasta as directed on package, adding spinach to the boiling water the last minute.

2. **COOK** and stir chicken and basil in large nonstick skillet sprayed with cooking spray on medium-high heat 3 min. Stir in spaghetti sauce and tomatoes; bring to boil. Simmer on low heat 3 min. or until chicken is done. Stir in Neufchâtel.

3. **DRAIN** pasta mixture; return to pan. Stir in chicken mixture and ½ cup mozzarella. Spoon into 2-qt. casserole or 8-inch square baking dish.

4. **BAKE** 20 min.; top with remaining cheeses. Bake 3 min. or until mozzarella is melted.

SERVING SUGGESTION:
Serve with CRYSTAL LIGHT Iced Tea.

easy shepherd's pie

PREP: 10 min. | TOTAL: 30 min. | MAKES: 6 servings.

▸ what you need!

1 lb. ground beef

2 cups hot mashed potatoes

4 oz. (½ of 8-oz. pkg.) PHILADELPHIA Cream Cheese, cubed

1 cup KRAFT Shredded Cheddar Cheese, divided

2 cloves garlic, minced

4 cups frozen mixed vegetables, thawed

1 cup beef gravy

▸ make it!

HEAT oven to 375°F.

1. **BROWN** meat in large skillet; drain.

2. **MEANWHILE,** mix potatoes, cream cheese, ½ cup Cheddar and garlic until well blended.

3. **ADD** vegetables and gravy to meat; mix well. Spoon into 9-inch square baking dish.

4. **COVER** with potato mixture and remaining Cheddar. Bake 20 min. or until heated through.

HEALTHY LIVING:
Save 70 calories and 9 grams of fat, including 5 grams of saturated fat, per serving by preparing with extra-lean ground beef, PHILADELPHIA Neufchâtel Cheese and KRAFT 2% Milk Shredded Cheddar Cheese.

BARBECUE SHEPHERD'S PIE:
Prepare omitting the garlic and substituting ¾ cup KRAFT Original Barbecue Sauce mixed with ½ tsp. onion powder for tho gravy.

CREATIVE LEFTOVERS:
This recipe is a great way to use leftover mashed potatoes.

mexican chicken casserole

PREP: 20 min. | **TOTAL: 45 min.** | **MAKES: 4 servings.**

▸ what you need!

¾ lb. boneless skinless chicken breasts, cut into bite-size pieces

1 tsp. ground cumin

1 green pepper, chopped

1½ cups TACO BELL® HOME ORIGINALS® Thick 'N Chunky Salsa

2 oz. (¼ of 8-oz. pkg.) PHILADELPHIA Neufchâtel Cheese, cubed

1 can (15 oz.) no-salt-added black beans, rinsed

1 tomato, chopped

2 whole wheat tortillas (6 inch)

½ cup KRAFT Mexican Style 2% Milk Finely Shredded Four Cheese, divided

▸ make it!

HEAT oven to 375°F.

1. **COOK** and stir chicken and cumin in nonstick skillet sprayed with cooking spray on medium heat 2 min. Add peppers; cook 2 min., stirring occasionally. Stir in salsa; cook 2 min. Add Neufchâtel; cook 2 min. or until melted. Stir in beans and tomatoes.

2. **SPOON** ⅓ of the chicken mixture into 8-inch square baking dish; cover with 1 tortilla and half each of the remaining chicken mixture and shredded cheese. Top with remaining tortilla and chicken mixture; cover.

3. **BAKE** 20 min. or until heated through. Sprinkle with remaining shredded cheese; bake, uncovered, 5 min. or until melted.

SPECIAL EXTRA:
Sprinkle with ¼ cup chopped cilantro just before serving.

creamy chicken pot pie

PREP: 10 min. | **TOTAL:** 40 min. | **MAKES:** 8 servings.

▶ what you need!

1   pkg. (8 oz.) PHILADELPHIA Cream Cheese, cubed

½   cup chicken broth

3   cups chopped cooked chicken

1   pkg. (16 oz.) frozen mixed vegetables, thawed

½   tsp. garlic salt

1   egg

½   cup milk

1   cup all-purpose baking mix

▶ make it!

HEAT oven to 400°F.

1. **COOK** cream cheese and broth in large saucepan on low heat until cream cheese is completely melted and mixture is well blended, stirring frequently with whisk. Stir in chicken, vegetables and garlic salt.

2. **SPOON** into 2-qt. casserole. Beat egg and milk in medium bowl with whisk until well blended; stir in baking mix just until moistened. Spoon over chicken mixture. Place casserole on baking sheet.

3. **BAKE** 25 to 30 min. or until golden brown.

SUBSTITUTE:
Prepare using PHILADELPHIA Neufchâtel Cheese.

SUBSTITUTE:
Substitute turkey for the chicken.

SERVING SUGGESTION:
For added color and texture, serve with a mixed green salad tossed with your favorite KRAFT Light Dressing.

Entrées

Easy pork, chicken and seafood dishes

tandoori chicken kabobs

PREP: 10 min. | TOTAL: 50 min. (incl. marinating) | MAKES: 4 servings.

▸ what you need!

2 oz. (¼ of 8-oz. pkg.) PHILADELPHIA Cream Cheese, softened

2 Tbsp. tandoori paste

1 lb. boneless skinless chicken breasts, cut into 2-inch pieces

▸ make it!

1. **MIX** cream cheese and tandoori paste in medium bowl. Add chicken; toss to coat. Refrigerate 30 min. to marinate.

2. **HEAT** broiler. Remove chicken from marinade; reserve marinade. Thread chicken onto 4 skewers; brush with reserved marinade. Place on rack of broiler pan.

3. **BROIL,** 6 inches from heat source, 8 to 10 min. or until chicken is done, turning after 5 min.

NOTE:
If using wooden skewers, soak skewers in water 30 min. before using to prevent the skewers from burning on the grill.

SERVING SUGGESTION:
Serve over hot cooked basmati rice with a mixed green salad.

parmesan-crusted chicken in cream sauce

PREP: 15 min. | TOTAL: 30 min. | MAKES: 4 servings.

▶ what you need!

2 cups instant brown rice, uncooked

1 can (14 oz.) fat-free reduced-sodium chicken broth, divided

6 RITZ Crackers, finely crushed (about ½ cup)

2 Tbsp. KRAFT Grated Parmesan Cheese

4 small boneless skinless chicken breast halves (1 lb.)

2 tsp. oil

⅓ cup PHILADELPHIA Chive & Onion ⅓ Less Fat than Cream Cheese

¾ lb. asparagus spears, trimmed, steamed

▶ make it!

1. **COOK** rice as directed on package, using 1¼ cups of the broth and ½ cup water.

2. **MEANWHILE,** mix cracker crumbs and Parmesan on plate. Rinse chicken with cold water; gently shake off excess. Dip chicken in crumb mixture, turning to evenly coat both sides of each breast. Discard any remaining crumb mixture.

3. **HEAT** oil in large nonstick skillet on medium heat. Add chicken; cook 5 to 6 min. on each side or until done (165°F). Transfer to plate; cover to keep warm. Add remaining broth and reduced-fat cream cheese to skillet; bring just to boil, stirring constantly. Cook 3 min. or until thickened, stirring frequently; spoon over chicken. Serve with rice and asparagus.

VARIATION:
Prepare using plain PHILADELPHIA ⅓ Less Fat than Cream Cheese and stirring in 1 Tbsp. chopped fresh chives along with the cream cheese.

chicken parmesan bundles

PREP: 35 min. | TOTAL: 1 hour 5 min. | MAKES: 6 servings.

▸ what you need!

4 oz. (½ of 8-oz. pkg.) PHILADELPHIA Cream Cheese, softened

1 pkg. (10 oz.) frozen chopped spinach, thawed, well drained

1¼ cups KRAFT Shredded Low-Moisture Part-Skim Mozzarella Cheese, divided

6 Tbsp. KRAFT Grated Parmesan Cheese, divided

6 small boneless skinless chicken breast halves (1½ lb.), pounded to ¼-inch thickness

1 egg

10 RITZ Crackers, crushed (about ½ cup)

1½ cups spaghetti sauce, heated

▸ make it!

HEAT oven to 375°F.

1. **MIX** cream cheese, spinach, 1 cup mozzarella and 3 Tbsp. Parmesan until well blended; spread onto chicken breasts. Starting at 1 short end of each breast, roll up chicken tightly. Secure with wooden toothpicks, if desired.

2. **BEAT** egg in shallow dish. Mix remaining Parmesan and cracker crumbs in separate shallow dish. Dip chicken in egg, then roll in crumb mixture. Place, seam-sides down, in 13×9-inch baking dish sprayed with cooking spray.

3. **BAKE** 30 min. or until chicken is done (165°F). Remove and discard toothpicks, if using. Serve topped with spaghetti sauce and remaining mozzarella.

HEALTHY LIVING:
Save 40 calories and 4 grams of fat per serving by preparing with PHILADELPHIA Neufchâtel Cheese, KRAFT 2% Milk Shredded Mozzarella Cheese and RITZ Reduced Fat Crackers.

MAKE AHEAD:
Assemble chicken bundles and place in baking dish as directed. Refrigerate up to 4 hours. When ready to serve, uncover and bake at 375°F for 35 min. or until chicken is done.

chicken in creamy pan sauce

PREP: 10 min. | **TOTAL: 30 min.** | **MAKES: 4 servings.**

▶ what you need!

4 small boneless skinless chicken breast halves (1 lb.)

2 Tbsp. flour

1 Tbsp. oil

¾ cup fat-free reduced-sodium chicken broth

4 oz. (½ of 8-oz. pkg.) PHILADELPHIA Cream Cheese, cubed

1 Tbsp. chopped fresh parsley

▶ make it!

1. **COAT** chicken with flour. Heat oil in large skillet on medium heat. Add chicken; cook 5 to 6 min. on each side or until done (165°F). Remove chicken from skillet, reserving drippings in skillet. Cover chicken to keep warm.

2. **ADD** broth to skillet; stir to scrape up browned bits from bottom of skillet. Add cream cheese; cook 2 to 3 min. or until cream cheese is melted and sauce starts to thicken, stirring constantly with whisk.

3. **RETURN** chicken to skillet; turn over to coat both sides of chicken with sauce. Cook 2 min. or until chicken is heated through. Sprinkle with parsley.

SPECIAL EXTRA:
Prepare recipe as directed. Transfer chicken to serving platter; top with 1 cup quartered cherry tomatoes. Drizzle with sauce; sprinkle with fresh basil.

NOTE:
If possible, use a large skillet with sloping sides when preparing this recipe. Not only does this allow you to easily turn the chicken pieces but the larger surface area speeds up the evaporation of the cooking liquids which, in turn, allows the chicken to brown more quickly.

fiesta chicken enchiladas

PREP: 15 min. | TOTAL: 35 min. | MAKES: 4 servings.

▸ what you need!

- 1 small onion, chopped
- 1 clove garlic, minced
- 4 cooked small boneless skinless chicken breasts (1 lb.), shredded
- 1 cup TACO BELL® HOME ORIGINALS® Thick 'N Chunky Salsa, divided
- 4 oz. (½ of 8-oz. pkg.) PHILADELPHIA Cream Cheese, cubed
- 1 Tbsp. chopped cilantro
- 1 tsp. ground cumin
- 1 cup KRAFT Shredded Cheddar & Monterey Jack Cheese, divided
- 8 flour tortillas (6 inch)

▸ make it!

HEAT oven to 350°F.

1. **HEAT** large skillet spayed with cooking spray on medium heat. Add onions and garlic; cook and stir 2 min. Add chicken, ¼ cup salsa, cream cheese, cilantro and cumin; mix well. Cook until heated through, stirring occasionally. Add ½ cup shredded cheese; mix well.

2. **SPOON** about ⅓ cup chicken mixture down center of each tortilla; roll up. Place, seam-sides down, in 13×9-inch baking dish sprayed with cooking spray; top with remaining salsa and shredded cheese.

3. **BAKE** 15 to 20 min. or until heated through.

SHORTCUT:
Substitute 2 pkg. (6 oz. each) OSCAR MAYER Deli Fresh Oven Roasted Chicken Breast Cuts for the shredded cooked fresh chicken.

TACO BELL® and HOME ORIGINALS® are trademarks owned and licensed by Taco Bell Corp.

creamy rice, chicken & spinach dinner

PREP: 10 min. | TOTAL: 40 min. | MAKES: 4 servings, 1½ cups each.

▶ what you need!

¼ cup KRAFT Roasted Red Pepper Italian with Parmesan Dressing

1 lb. boneless skinless chicken breasts, cut into strips

1½ cups fat-free reduced-sodium chicken broth

2 cups instant brown rice, uncooked

4 oz. (½ of 8-oz. pkg.) PHILADELPHIA Neufchâtel Cheese, cubed

1 pkg. (8 oz.) baby spinach leaves

1 large tomato, chopped

2 Tbsp. KRAFT Grated Parmesan Cheese

▶ make it!

1. **HEAT** dressing in Dutch oven or large deep skillet on medium-high heat. Add chicken; cook 3 min. Stir in broth; bring to boil. Add rice; stir. Return to boil; cover. Simmer on medium heat 5 min.

2. **ADD** Neufchâtel; cook 2 to 3 min. or until melted, stirring frequently. Add spinach. (Pan will be full.) Cook, covered, 1 min. or until spinach is wilted. Stir gently to mix in spinach.

3. **REMOVE** pan from heat. Let stand, covered, 5 min. Stir in tomatoes; top with Parmesan.

SUBSTITUTE:
Prepare using KRAFT Light Zesty Italian Dressing.

farmhouse chicken dinner

PREP: 15 min. | TOTAL: 50 min. | MAKES: 4 servings.

▶ what you need!

¼ cup flour

½ tsp. black pepper

4 small bone-in chicken breast halves (1½ lb.), skin removed

¼ cup KRAFT Light Zesty Italian Dressing

2 cups baby carrots

1 onion, cut into wedges

1 can (14½ oz.) fat-free reduced-sodium chicken broth, divided

2 cups instant brown rice, uncooked

4 oz. (½ of 8-oz. pkg.) PHILADELPHIA Neufchâtel Cheese, cubed

2 Tbsp. chopped fresh parsley

▶ make it!

1. **MIX** flour and pepper in shallow dish. Add chicken; turn to coat both sides of each piece. Gently shake off excess flour. Heat dressing in large nonstick skillet on medium heat. Add chicken, meat-sides down; cook 5 to 6 min. or until golden brown. Turn chicken. Add carrots, onions and 1 cup broth; cover. Simmer on medium-low heat 20 min. or until chicken is done (165°F).

2. **MEANWHILE,** cook rice as directed on package; spoon onto platter. Use slotted spoon to remove chicken and vegetables from skillet; place over rice. Cover to keep warm.

3. **ADD** Neufchâtel and remaining broth to skillet; cook on high heat until Neufchâtel is melted and sauce is well blended, stirring constantly. Simmer on medium-low heat 3 to 5 min. or until slightly thickened, stirring occasionally. Spoon over chicken and vegetables; top with parsley.

SUBSTITUTE:
Substitute 8 bone-in chicken thighs with skin removed for the chicken breasts. Prepare as directed, cooking until chicken is done (165°F).

tuscan chicken simmer

PREP: 5 min. | TOTAL: 25 min. | MAKES: 4 servings.

▶ what you need!

4 small boneless skinless chicken breast halves (1 lb.)

4 oz. (½ of 8-oz. pkg.) PHILADELPHIA Cream Cheese, cubed

¼ cup water

¼ cup pesto

2 cups grape or cherry tomatoes

1 cup KRAFT Finely Shredded Italian* Five Cheese Blend

▶ make it!

1. **HEAT** large nonstick skillet sprayed with cooking spray on medium-high heat. Add chicken; cover. Cook 5 to 7 min. on each side or until done (165°F). Remove chicken from skillet; cover to keep warm.

2. **ADD** cream cheese, water, pesto and tomatoes to skillet. Cook, uncovered, on medium heat 2 min. or until cream cheese is melted and mixture is well blended, stirring occasionally.

3. **RETURN** chicken to skillet. Cook and stir 1 min. or until chicken is coated and heated through. Sprinkle with shredded cheese.

HEALTHY LIVING:
Save 50 calories and 5 grams of fat per serving by preparing with PHILADELPHIA Neufchâtel Cheese and KRAFT 2% Milk Shredded Mozzarella Cheese.

SERVING SUGGESTION:
Spoon over hot cooked ravioli or fettuccine.

* Made with quality cheeses crafted in the USA

cheesy chicken tostadas

PREP: 10 min. | **TOTAL: 17 min.** | **MAKES: 6 servings.**

▶ what you need!

- 6 tostada shells
- ½ cup (½ of 8-oz. tub) PHILADELPHIA Chive & Onion Cream Cheese Spread
- ¾ lb. cooked chicken, shredded
- 6 KRAFT Singles
- 1 avocado, sliced
- 1½ cups shredded lettuce
- 1 tomato, chopped

▶ make it!

HEAT oven to 375°F.

1. **PLACE** tostada shells on baking sheet; spread with cream cheese spread. Fill with chicken and Singles.

2. **BAKE** 5 to 7 min. or until heated through.

3. **TOP** with remaining ingredients.

SIZE-WISE:
Looking for something to serve at your next Cinco de Mayo celebration? This tasty dish makes enough for 6 servings.

SUBSTITUTE:
Substitute shredded cooked beef or pork for the chicken.

creamy thai green curry chicken & rice

PREP: 15 min. | TOTAL: 30 min. | MAKES: 4 servings, 2 cups each.

▶ what you need!

1 Tbsp. canola oil

2 Tbsp. green curry paste

1 lb. boneless skinless chicken breasts, cut into bite-size pieces

1 small onion, thinly sliced

1 each red and green bell pepper, cut into thin strips, then cut crosswise in half

4 oz. (½ of 8-oz. pkg.) PHILADELPHIA Cream Cheese, cubed

¼ cup milk

⅛ tsp. white pepper

4 cups hot cooked long-grain white rice

▶ make it!

1. **HEAT** oil in large nonstick skillet on medium heat. Stir in curry paste until well blended. Add chicken and onions; cook and stir 6 to 8 min. or until chicken is done. Stir in bell peppers; cook 4 to 5 min. or until crisp-tender.

2. **ADD** cream cheese, milk and white pepper; cook until cream cheese is melted and evenly coats chicken and vegetables, stirring frequently.

3. **SERVE** over rice.

SUBSTITUTE:
Prepare using red curry paste.

roast pork tenderloin supper

PREP: 20 min. | TOTAL: 45 min. | MAKES: 6 servings.

▶ what you need!

2 pork tenderloins (1½ lb.)

¼ cup GREY POUPON Dijon Mustard

2 tsp. dried thyme leaves

1 pkg. (6 oz.) STOVE TOP Stuffing Mix for Chicken

½ cup fat-free reduced-sodium chicken broth

4 oz. (½ of 8-oz. pkg.) PHILADELPHIA Neufchâtel Cheese, cubed

1 lb. fresh green beans, trimmed, steamed

▶ make it!

HEAT oven to 400°F.

1. **HEAT** large nonstick skillet on medium heat. Add meat; cook 5 min. or until browned on all sides, turning occasionally. Remove meat from skillet, reserving meat drippings in skillet; place meat in 13×9-inch baking dish. Mix mustard and thyme; spread onto meat.

2. **BAKE** 20 to 25 min. or until meat is done (160°F). Transfer to carving board; tent with foil. Let stand 5 min. Meanwhile, prepare stuffing as directed on package, reducing the spread to 1 Tbsp.

3. **ADD** broth to same skillet. Bring to boil on high heat. Reduce heat to medium-low. Add Neufchâtel; cook 2 min. or until Neufchâtel is completely melted and mixture is well blended, stirring constantly.

4. **CUT** meat into thin slices. Serve topped with the Neufchâtel sauce along with the stuffing and beans.

NOTE:
If you purchased the broth in a 32-oz. pkg., store remaining broth In refrigerator up to 1 week. Or if you purchased a 14-oz. can, pour the remaining broth into a glass container; store in refrigerator up to 1 week.

NUTRITION BONUS:
This oh-so-easy, low-calorie dinner features foods from three different food groups, helping you to eat a variety of foods.

curried pork and noodles

PREP: 35 min. | MAKES: 6 servings, ¾ cup meat mixture and ¾ cup pasta each.

▶ what you need!

4 slices OSCAR MAYER Bacon, chopped

½ cup milk

4 oz. (½ of 8-oz. pkg.) PHILADELPHIA Cream Cheese, cubed

¾ cup BAKER'S ANGEL FLAKE Coconut

1 tsp. curry powder

½ tsp. ground red pepper (cayenne)

½ lb. spaghetti, uncooked

1½ lb. pork tenderloin, cut into bite-size pieces

1 red or green bell pepper, cut into strips

2 green onions, sliced

▶ make it!

1. **COOK** bacon in large skillet on medium-high heat 5 min. or until crisp; remove to paper towels to drain. Discard drippings. Blend milk, cream cheese, coconut and seasonings in blender until smooth. Cook spaghetti as directed on package.

2. **MEANWHILE,** cook half the tenderloin pieces in same skillet on medium-low heat 4 min. or until evenly browned, stirring frequently. Transfer to bowl; cover to keep warm. Repeat with remaining tenderloin pieces. Add bell peppers to skillet; cook and stir 3 min. Return tenderloin meat to skillet along with cream cheese mixture; cook on low heat 8 to 10 min. or until meat is done, stirring occasionally.

3. **DRAIN** spaghetti; place on platter. Top with meat mixture, bacon and onions.

SERVING SUGGESTION:
Serve with a refreshing cucumber salad to help tame the heat of the curried pork.

skillet beef picadillo with walnut sauce

PREP: 10 min. | TOTAL: 40 min. | MAKES: 6 servings.

▶ what you need!

2 Tbsp. KRAFT Zesty Italian Dressing

1 cup sliced onions

1 clove garlic, minced

1½ lb. lean ground beef

¾ lb. cooked new potatoes (about 7), cut into ½-inch cubes

4 poblano chiles, roasted, peeled, seeded and cut into strips

1 can (8 oz.) tomato sauce

½ cup milk

4 oz. (½ of 8-oz. pkg.) PHILADELPHIA Cream Cheese, softened

½ cup chopped PLANTERS Walnuts

▶ make it!

1. **HEAT** dressing in large skillet on medium heat. Add onions and garlic; cook 3 min. or until onions are tender, stirring occasionally. Stir in meat; cook 8 to 10 min. or until meat is browned, stirring occasionally.

2. **STIR** in potatoes, chiles and tomato sauce; cover. Simmer on medium-low heat 15 min.

3. **MEANWHILE,** blend remaining ingredients in blender until well blended. Serve spooned over meat mixture.

SERVING SUGGESTION:
Serve with a mixed green salad tossed with KRAFT Light Ranch Dressing.

20-minute skillet salmon

PREP: 10 min. | TOTAL: 20 min. | MAKES: 4 servings.

▶ what you need!

1 Tbsp. oil

4 salmon fillets (1 lb.)

1 cup fat-free milk

½ cup (½ of 8-oz. tub) PHILADELPHIA ⅓ Less Fat than Cream Cheese

½ cup chopped cucumbers

2 Tbsp. chopped fresh dill

▶ make it!

1. **HEAT** oil in large skillet on medium-high heat. Add fish; cook 5 min. on each side or until fish flakes easily with fork. Remove from skillet; cover to keep warm.

2. **ADD** milk and reduced-fat cream cheese to skillet; cook and stir until cream cheese is completely melted and mixture is well blended. Stir in cucumbers and dill.

3. **RETURN** fish to skillet. Cook 2 min. or until heated through. Serve topped with cream cheese sauce.

SERVING SUGGESTION:
Round out the meal with hot cooked rice and steamed vegetables. Or serve salmon on a bed of salad greens.

COOKING KNOW-HOW:
When salmon is done, it will appear opaque and flake easily with fork.

FOOD FACTS:
Check salmon fillets for bones before cooking by running fingers over surface. Small bumps are usually a sign of bones—use tweezers to remove them.

fish in roasted red pepper sauce

PREP: 10 min. | TOTAL: 30 min. | MAKES: 4 servings.

▶ what you need!

4 cod fillets (1 lb.)

¼ cup flour

¼ cup KRAFT Zesty Italian Dressing

½ cup sliced onions

2 oz. (¼ of 8-oz. pkg.) PHILADELPHIA Cream Cheese, softened

¼ cup roasted red peppers

¼ cup chicken broth

1 clove garlic, peeled

2 Tbsp. chopped cilantro

▶ make it!

1. **COAT** both sides of fish with flour; set aside. Heat dressing in large skillet on medium-high heat. Add onions; cook and stir until crisp-tender. Add fish; cook 5 to 7 min. on each side or until fish flakes easily with fork.

2. **MEANWHILE,** blend cream cheese, peppers, broth and garlic in blender until smooth. Spoon into medium saucepan. Bring to boil on medium-high heat; simmer on low heat 5 min., stirring occasionally.

3. **PLACE** fish on serving platter; top with onions and cream cheese mixture. Sprinkle with cilantro.

MAKE IT EASY:
Substitute jarred roasted red peppers for the roasted fresh red peppers.

BUYING AND STORING FROZEN FISH & SHELLFISH:
When purchasing frozen fish or shellfish, make sure it is well wrapped and solidly frozen, with no odor. Always check the "sell-by" date on the package. Avoid fish that has been thawed and refrozen. Store it in the refrigerator, tightly wrapped, for up to 2 days. Never refreeze fish or shellfish once it's been thawed.

swordfish with leek cream

PREP: 15 min. | TOTAL: 23 min. | MAKES: 4 servings.

▶ what you need!

4 swordfish steaks (1 lb.)

2 Tbsp. oil

2 Tbsp. butter or margarine

1 leek, cut into 1-inch strips

4 oz. (½ of 8-oz. pkg.) PHILADELPHIA Cream Cheese, cubed

3 Tbsp. dry white wine

½ cup milk

2 Tbsp. chopped fresh parsley

½ tsp. garlic salt

¼ tsp. black pepper

▶ make it!

HEAT greased grill to high heat.

1. **BRUSH** fish with oil. Grill 3 to 4 min. on each side or until fish flakes easily with fork.

2. **MEANWHILE,** melt butter in medium skillet on medium heat. Add leeks; cook and stir until tender. Add remaining ingredients; cook on low until cream cheese is melted and mixture is well blended, stirring frequently.

3. **SERVE** fish topped with sauce.

SERVING SUGGESTION:
Serve with a hot steamed vegetable and whole-grain rolls for an elegant dinner for 4.

SUBSTITUTE:
Prepare using PHILADELPHIA Neufchâtel Cheese.

Soups & Sandwiches

Simple meals made delicious with cream cheese

"croque monsieur"

PREP: 5 min. | TOTAL: 10 min | MAKES: 2 servings.

▸ what you need!

2 slices French or Italian bread (1-inch thick)

2 Tbsp. PHILADELPHIA Chive & Onion Cream Cheese Spread

12 slices OSCAR MAYER Deli Fresh Shaved Virginia Brand Ham

½ cup KRAFT Shredded Swiss Cheese

▸ make it!

HEAT broiler.

1. **BROIL** bread, 2 to 3 inches from heat, 30 sec. or until toasted. Turn over.

2. **SPREAD** with cream cheese spread; top with ham and Swiss cheese.

3. **BROIL** 30 sec. or until cheese is melted.

SERVING SUGGESTION:
Serve with a crisp mixed green salad.

creamy corn and turkey soup

PREP: 10 min. | **TOTAL:** 25 min. | **MAKES:** 6 servings, 1 cup each.

▶ what you need!

½ cup chopped onions

1 red pepper, chopped, divided

2 Tbsp. butter or margarine

4 oz. (½ of 8-oz. pkg.) PHILADELPHIA Cream Cheese, cubed

1 can (14.75 oz.) cream-style corn

2 cups chicken broth

¾ cup milk

2 cups shredded cooked turkey

▶ make it!

1. **COOK** onions and half the peppers in butter in large saucepan on medium heat until crisp-tender, stirring frequently.

2. **ADD** cream cheese; cook on low heat until melted, stirring constantly. Stir in corn, broth, milk and turkey.

3. **COOK** until soup is heated through, stirring occasionally. Serve topped with remaining peppers.

SUBSTITUTE:
Prepare using PHILADELPHIA Neufchâtel Cheese.

NOTE:
This is a great way to use leftover cooked turkey.

creamy broccoli soup

PREP: 15 min. | **TOTAL:** 30 min. | **MAKES:** 6 servings, ¾ cup each.

▶ what you need!

¼ cup chopped onions

1 Tbsp. butter or margarine

1 Tbsp. flour

2 cups milk

4 oz. (½ of 8-oz. pkg.) PHILADELPHIA Cream Cheese, cubed

½ lb. (8 oz.) VELVEETA Pasteurized Prepared Cheese Product, cut into ½-inch cubes

1 pkg. (10 oz.) frozen chopped broccoli, cooked, drained

¼ tsp. ground nutmeg

⅛ tsp. black pepper

▶ make it!

1. **COOK** and stir onions in butter in 2-qt. saucepan on medium-high heat until onions are crisp-tender. Blend in flour.

2. **ADD** milk and cream cheese; cook on medium heat until cream cheese is melted, stirring frequently.

3. **STIR** in remaining ingredients; cook until heated through, stirring occasionally.

SUBSTITUTE:
Substitute frozen chopped spinach; frozen cauliflower florets, chopped; or frozen asparagus spears, chopped; for the broccoli.

USE YOUR MICROWAVE:
Microwave onions and butter in 2-qt. microwaveable bowl on HIGH 30 sec. or until onions are crisp-tender. Stir in flour and milk. Microwave 3 to 4 min. or until heated through, stirring every 2 min. Stir in cream cheese. Microwave 4 to 6 min. or until cream cheese is melted, stirring every 2 min. Stir in remaining ingredients. Microwave 30 sec. or until heated through.

santa fe chicken fajita soup

PREP: 15 min. | TOTAL: 1 hour 5 min. (incl. refrigerating) | MAKES: 8 servings, 1 cup each.

▶ what you need!

1 pkg. (1.4 oz.) TACO BELL® HOME ORIGINALS® Fajita Seasoning Mix

⅓ cup water

1 lb. boneless skinless chicken breasts, cut into thin strips

4 large cloves garlic, minced

2 Tbsp. chopped fresh cilantro

1 large red onion, chopped

1 small green bell pepper, chopped

1 pkg. (8 oz.) PHILADELPHIA Fat Free Cream Cheese, cut into cubes

1 lb. (16 oz.) VELVEETA 2% Milk Pasteurized Prepared Cheese Product, cut into ½-inch cubes

2 cans (14.5 oz. each) fat-free reduced-sodium chicken broth

▶ make it!

1. **COMBINE** seasoning mix and water in medium bowl. Add chicken; toss to evenly coat. Refrigerate 30 min.

2. **COOK** garlic and cilantro in large nonstick saucepan sprayed with cooking spray on medium-high heat 1 min. Stir in chicken mixture, onions and peppers; cook 10 min. or until chicken is done, stirring frequently.

3. **ADD** cream cheese, VELVEETA and broth; mix well. Cook on medium heat until cream cheese and VELVEETA are completely melted and soup is heated through, stirring occasionally.

SERVING SUGGESTION:
Serve this hearty main-dish soup with a tossed leafy green salad.

SPECIAL EXTRA:
Garnish with additional chopped cilantro just before serving.

TACO BELL® and HOME ORIGINALS® are trademarks owned and licensed by Taco Bell Corp.

potato leek soup

PREP: 20 min. | TOTAL: 1 hour | MAKES: 8 servings, 1 cup each.

▶ what you need!

2 Tbsp. olive oil

4 large leeks (about 2 lb.), cut into ¼-inch-thick slices

4 large baking potatoes, peeled, cubed (about 4 cups)

1¼ qt. (5 cups) water

1 tsp. salt

½ tsp. black pepper

1 pkg. (8 oz.) PHILADELPHIA Cream Cheese, cubed

½ cup milk

¼ cup chopped fresh chives

▶ make it!

1. **HEAT** oil in Dutch oven on medium heat. Add leeks; cook 5 min. or until tender, stirring occasionally. Add potatoes, water, salt and pepper; cover. Bring to boil; simmer on medium-low heat 15 to 20 min. or until potatoes are tender. Cool 10 min.

2. **ADD** leek mixture, in batches, to blender; blend until puréed. Return to Dutch oven. Whisk in cream cheese, a few cubes at a time; cook on medium heat until cream cheese is completely melted, stirring constantly.

3. **ADD** milk; cook until heated through, stirring occasionally. Sprinkle with chives and additional pepper, if desired. Serve with PREMIUM Multigrain Saltine Crackers.

SIZE-WISE:
Savor every spoonful of this indulgent soup. One serving goes a long way on flavor.

PREPARING LEEKS:
Leeks are grown in sandy soil and must be washed well before using. To prepare leeks, trim the roots and remove the dark green portions. Only the white portion of the leek is used. Chop or slice the white sections, then rinse in water to remove any soil or sand.

clam chowder

PREP: 15 min. | TOTAL: 40 min. | MAKES: 5 servings, 1 cup each.

▸ what you need!

1 small onion, chopped

1 stalk celery, chopped

2 slices OSCAR MAYER Bacon, chopped

1 lb. red potatoes (about 2), peeled, cut into ¼-inch cubes

1½ cups water

1 cup milk

4 oz. (½ of 8-oz. pkg.) PHILADELPHIA Cream Cheese, cubed

1 can (6¼ oz.) minced clams, undrained

▸ make it!

1. **COOK** and stir onions, celery and bacon in medium saucepan on medium heat 5 min. or until vegetables are crisp-tender. Add potatoes and water; bring to boil. Cook 15 min. or until potatoes are tender.

2. **MICROWAVE** milk and cream cheese in small microwaveable bowl on HIGH 1½ min. or until milk is heated through. Whisk until cream cheese is completely melted and mixture is well blended. Add to potato mixture.

3. **STIR** in clams; cook 2 min. or until heated through, stirring frequently. (Do not boil.)

SUBSTITUTE:
Prepare using PHILADELPHIA Neufchâtel Cheese.

stuffed fiesta burgers

PREP: 15 min. | TOTAL: 33 min. | MAKES: 4 servings.

▸ what you need!

1 lb. ground beef

1 pkg. (1¼ oz.) TACO BELL® HOME ORIGINALS® Taco Seasoning Mix

¼ cup PHILADELPHIA Chive & Onion Cream Cheese Spread

⅓ cup KRAFT Shredded Cheddar Cheese

4 hamburger buns, lightly toasted

½ cup TACO BELL® HOME ORIGINALS® Thick 'N Chunky Medium Salsa

1 avocado, cut into 8 slices

▸ make it!

HEAT grill to medium heat.

1. **MIX** meat and seasoning mix; shape into 8 thin patties. Mix cream cheese spread and Cheddar; spoon about 2 Tbsp. onto center of each of 4 patties. Top with remaining patties; pinch edges together to seal.

2. **GRILL** 7 to 9 min. on each side or until burgers are done (160°F.)

3. **FILL** buns with burgers, salsa and avocados.

SUBSTITUTE:
Substitute thawed LOUIS RICH Pure Ground Turkey for the ground beef.

FUN IDEA:
With the wide variety of salsas now available, why not try topping these burgers with a roasted corn salsa, green salsa or even a fruit salsa?

TACO BELL® and HOME ORIGINALS® are trademarks owned and licensed by Taco Bell Corp.

wrapped veggie sandwich

PREP: 5 min. | MAKES: 1 serving, 2 roll-ups.

▶ what you need!

2 flour tortillas (6 inch)

2 Tbsp. PHILADELPHIA Chive & Onion Cream Cheese Spread

1 KRAFT Singles, cut in half

1 cup fresh spinach leaves

½ cup chopped, drained roasted red peppers

¼ cup shredded carrots

▶ make it!

1. **SPREAD** tortillas with cream cheese spread.

2. **TOP** with remaining ingredients; roll up.

3. **SECURE** with toothpicks.

SUBSTITUTE:
Use PHILADELPHIA Roasted Garlic Light Cream Cheese Spread.

terrific tuna melt

PREP: 5 min. | TOTAL: 8 min. | MAKES: 1 serving.

▶ what you need!

2 Tbsp. PHILADELPHIA Chive & Onion Cream Cheese Spread

1 can (3 oz.) white tuna in water, drained, flaked (about ¼ cup)

1 pita bread

3 Tbsp. KRAFT Shredded Mild Cheddar Cheese

1 Tbsp. finely chopped mixed fresh vegetables (cucumbers, carrots, radishes)

▶ make it!

HEAT oven or toaster oven to 400°F.

1. **MIX** cream cheese spread and tuna; spread onto bread. Top with Cheddar.

2. **BAKE** 2 to 3 min. or until Cheddar is melted.

3. **TOP** with vegetables.

VARIATION:
Prepare as directed, substituting 1 KRAFT Deli Fresh Mild Cheddar Cheese Slice for the shredded cheese and/or 1 toasted multi-grain bread slice for the pita bread.

FOOD FACTS:
Flatbread can be substituted for the pita bread in this recipe. Since it is typically softer than pita bread, it may need to be toasted before topping with the remaining ingredients as directed.

SERVING SUGGESTION:
Serve with a side salad and fresh fruit to round out the meal.

creamy roast beef sandwiches

PREP: 25 min. | TOTAL: 35 min. | MAKES: 6 servings, 2 filled pita halves each.

▶ what you need!

1 cup sliced onions, separated into rings

1 Tbsp. butter or margarine

6 oz. (¾ of 8-oz. pkg.) PHILADELPHIA Cream Cheese, cubed

½ cup milk

1 Tbsp. KRAFT Prepared Horseradish

6 pita breads, cut in half

1 lb. shaved deli roast beef

2 tomatoes, chopped

2 cups shredded lettuce

▶ make it!

1. **COOK** and stir onions in butter in medium skillet on medium heat until tender. Add cream cheese and milk. Cook on low heat until cream cheese is completely melted and mixture is well blended, stirring occasionally. Stir in horseradish.

2. **FILL** pita pockets with meat, tomatoes and lettuce.

3. **DRIZZLE** with horseradish sauce.

SERVING SUGGESTION:
Pair this recipe with your favorite fresh fruit and a glass of fat-free milk.

VARIATION:
Prepare sauce as directed. Refrigerate 1 hour or until ready to serve. Serve cold with the sandwiches.

garden vegetable grill sandwich

PREP: 10 min. | TOTAL: 22 min. | MAKES: 4 servings.

▶ what you need!

2 slices red onion (¼-inch thick)

2 portobello mushroom caps (4 inch)

4 slices zucchini (½-inch thick)

¼ cup KRAFT Balsamic Vinaigrette Dressing

4 whole wheat rolls, split

¼ cup PHILADELPHIA Garden Vegetable ⅓ Less Fat than Cream Cheese

1 tomato, cut into 4 slices

4 KRAFT 2% Milk Pepperjack Singles

▶ make it!

HEAT grill to medium heat.

1. **GRILL** vegetables 5 to 7 min or until crisp-tender, turning and brushing occasionally with dressing. Meanwhile, grill rolls, cut-sides down, 1 to 2 min. or until lightly toasted.

2. **REMOVE** vegetables and rolls from grill. Cut mushrooms into thin strips. Separate onions into rings.

3. **SPREAD** rolls with cream cheese; fill with grilled vegetables, tomatoes and 2% Milk Singles.

HOW TO GRILL ONIONS:
Thread onion slices onto 2 skewers before grilling to prevent the slices from separating into rings when grilling.

Side Dishes

Perfect accompaniments to any meal

new potatoes in dill cream sauce

PREP: 10 min. | TOTAL: 30 min. | MAKES: 16 servings, about ½ cup each.

▶ what you need!

2½ lb. new potatoes (about 20), quartered

1 tub (8 oz.) PHILADELPHIA Chive & Onion Cream Cheese Spread

¼ cup milk

1 green pepper, chopped

3 Tbsp. chopped fresh dill

▶ make it!

1. **COOK** potatoes in boiling water in saucepan on medium heat 15 min. or until potatoes are tender; drain.

2. **MEANWHILE,** microwave cream cheese spread, milk and peppers in large microwaveable bowl on HIGH 40 to 50 sec. or until cream cheese spread is melted when stirred. Stir in dill until well blended.

3. **ADD** potatoes; toss to coat.

SUBSTITUTE:
Substitute chopped fresh basil leaves or 2 tsp. dill weed for the chopped fresh dill.

CREATIVE LEFTOVERS:
Refrigerate any leftovers. Serve as a cold potato salad, stirring in a small amount of additional milk to thin, if necessary.

mashed potato layer bake

PREP: 40 min. | TOTAL: 1 hour | MAKES: 14 servings, ½ cup each.

▸ what you need!

3¼ lb. baking potatoes (about 7), peeled, chopped and cooked

½ lb. sweet potatoes (about 3), peeled, chopped and cooked

1 tub (8 oz.) PHILADELPHIA Chive & Onion Cream Cheese Spread, divided

½ cup BREAKSTONE'S or KNUDSEN Sour Cream, divided

¼ tsp. each salt and pepper, divided

¼ cup KRAFT Shredded or Grated Parmesan Cheese, divided

¼ cup KRAFT Shredded Cheddar Cheese, divided

▸ make it!

HEAT oven to 375°F.

1. **PLACE** potatoes in separate bowls. Add half each of the cream cheese spread and sour cream to each bowl; season with salt and pepper. Mash until creamy.

2. **STIR** half the Parmesan into white potatoes. Stir half the Cheddar into sweet potatoes. Layer half each of the potatoes in 2-qt. clear glass casserole. Repeat layers.

3. **BAKE** 15 min. Top with remaining cheeses; bake 5 min. or until melted.

MAKE AHEAD:
Assemble casserole as directed, but do not add the cheese topping. Refrigerate casserole and cheese topping separately up to 3 days. When ready to serve, bake casserole (uncovered) as directed, increasing baking time as needed until casserole is heated through. Top with remaining cheeses and continue as directed.

oat-topped sweet potato crisp

PREP: 20 min. | BAKE: 40 min. | MAKES: 8 servings.

▶ what you need!

1 pkg. (8 oz.) PHILADELPHIA Cream Cheese, softened

1 can (40 oz.) cut sweet potatoes, drained

¾ cup packed brown sugar, divided

¼ tsp. ground cinnamon

1 Granny Smith apple, chopped

⅔ cup chopped cranberries

½ cup flour

½ cup old-fashioned or quick-cooking oats, uncooked

⅓ cup cold butter or margarine

¼ cup chopped PLANTERS Pecans

▶ make it!

HEAT oven to 350°F.

1. **BEAT** cream cheese, potatoes, ¼ cup sugar and cinnamon with mixer until well blended. Spoon into 1½-qt. casserole; top with apples and cranberries.

2. **MIX** flour, oats and remaining sugar in medium bowl; cut in butter until mixture resembles coarse crumbs. Stir in nuts. Sprinkle over fruit layer in casserole.

3. **BAKE** 35 to 40 min. or until heated through.

SUBSTITUTE:
Prepare using PHILADELPHIA Neufchâtel Cheese.

garlic mashed potatoes

PREP: 10 min. | TOTAL: 30 min. | MAKES: 8 servings, about ½ cup each.

▶ what you need!

2½ lb. potatoes (about 7), peeled, quartered

4 cloves garlic, minced

1 tub (8 oz.) PHILADELPHIA Cream Cheese Spread

1 Tbsp. butter or margarine

1 tsp. salt

▶ make it!

1. **COOK** potatoes and garlic in boiling water in large saucepan 20 min. or until potatoes are tender; drain.

2. **MASH** potatoes until smooth.

3. **STIR** in remaining ingredients until well blended.

SERVING SUGGESTION:
Add contrast to the potatoes by serving them with a crisp mixed green salad or vegetable, and lean fish, meat or poultry.

FOOD FACTS:
For best results, use russet or red potatoes since they work best for mashing.

SUBSTITUTE:
Prepare using PHILADELPHIA Chive & Onion Cream Cheese Spread.

MAKE IT EASY:
Use mixer to beat potatoes instead of using a hand masher.

easy cheesy scalloped potatoes

PREP: 30 min. | TOTAL: 1 hour | MAKES: 15 servings, ¾ cup each.

▶ what you need!

1 pkg. (8 oz.) PHILADELPHIA Cream Cheese, softened

½ cup BREAKSTONE'S or KNUDSEN Sour Cream

1 cup chicken broth

3 lb. red potatoes (about 9), thinly sliced

1 pkg. (6 oz.) OSCAR MAYER Smoked Ham, chopped

1 pkg. (8 oz.) KRAFT Shredded Cheddar Cheese, divided

1 cup frozen peas

▶ make it!

HEAT oven to 350°F.

1. **MIX** cream cheese, sour cream and broth in large bowl until well blended. Add potatoes, ham, 1¾ cups Cheddar and peas; stir gently to evenly coat all ingredients.

2. **SPOON** into 13×9-inch baking dish sprayed with cooking spray; top with remaining Cheddar.

3. **BAKE** 1 hour or until casserole is heated through and potatoes are tender.

SERVING SUGGESTION:
Balance this creamy, indulgent side dish by serving it alongside cooked lean meat or fish and a steamed green vegetable.

PURCHASING POTATOES:
Look for firm, smooth, well-shaped potatoes that are free of wrinkles, cracks and blemishes. Avoid any with green-tinged skins or sprouting "eyes" or buds.

VARIATION:
Substitute OSCAR MAYER Smoked Turkey for the ham and/or 1 cup frozen mixed vegetables for the peas.

twice-baked sweet potatoes

PREP: 10 min. | TOTAL: 53 min. | MAKES: 4 servings.

▶ what you need!

2 large sweet potatoes

2 oz. (¼ of 8-oz. pkg.) PHILADELPHIA Neufchâtel Cheese, cubed

2 Tbsp. fat-free milk

1 Tbsp. brown sugar

¼ tsp. ground cinnamon

¼ cup chopped PLANTERS Pecans

▶ make it!

HEAT oven to 425°F.

1. **CUT** potatoes lengthwise in half; place, cut-sides down, in foil-lined 15×10×1-inch pan. Bake 30 to 35 min. or until tender.

2. **SCOOP** out centers of potatoes into bowl, leaving ¼-inch-thick shells. Add Neufchâtel, milk, sugar and cinnamon to potatoes; mash until blended.

3. **FILL** shells with potato mixture; top with nuts. Bake 8 min. or until potatoes are heated through and nuts are toasted.

SHORTCUT:
Pierce whole sweet potatoes with fork; wrap in damp paper towels. Microwave on HIGH 7 to 8 min. or until tender. Cut potatoes in half; scoop out centers and continue as directed.

MAKE AHEAD:
Stuff potato shells as directed; refrigerate up to 1 hour. When ready to serve, bake as directed, increasing baking time as needed until filling is heated through.

NUTRITION BONUS:
This classic side gets a twist by using sweet potatoes. Not only are the potatoes rich in vitamin A, but they're also a good source of fiber.

crust topped broccoli cheese bake

PREP: 10 min. | TOTAL: 40 min. | MAKES: 14 servings.

▶ what you need!

½ cup (½ of 8-oz. tub) PHILADELPHIA Chive & Onion Cream Cheese Spread

1 can (10¾ oz.) condensed cream of mushroom soup

½ cup water

2 pkg. (16 oz. each) frozen broccoli florets, thawed, drained

1 cup KRAFT Shredded Cheddar Cheese

1 thawed frozen puff pastry sheet (½ of 17.3-oz. pkg.)

1 egg, beaten

▶ make it!

HEAT oven to 400°F.

1. **MIX** cream cheese spread, soup and water in large bowl until well blended. Stir in broccoli and Cheddar. Spoon into 2½- to 3-qt. shallow rectangular or oval baking dish.

2. **ROLL** pastry sheet on lightly floured surface to fit top of baking dish. Cover dish completely with pastry. Press pastry edges against rim of dish to seal. Brush with egg; pierce with knife to vent.

3. **BAKE** 30 min. or until filling is heated through and pastry is puffed and golden brown.

MAKE AHEAD:
Casserole can be assembled in advance. Refrigerate up to 24 hours. When ready to serve, bake (uncovered) as directed.

VARIATION:
Prepare as directed, using PHILADELPHIA Chive & Onion ⅓ Less Fat than Cream Cheese and KRAFT 2% Milk Shredded Cheddar Cheese.

corn souffle

▶ what you need!

2 Tbsp. butter

1 pkg. (8 oz.) PHILADELPHIA Cream Cheese, cubed

1 can (15¼ oz.) whole kernel corn, drained

1 can (14.75 oz.) cream-style corn

1 pkg. (8.5 oz.) corn muffin mix

2 eggs, beaten

1 cup KRAFT Shredded Cheddar Cheese

▶ make it!

HEAT oven to 350°F.

1. **MICROWAVE** butter in medium microwaveable bowl on HIGH 30 sec. or until melted. Stir in cream cheese. Microwave 15 sec. or until cream cheese is softened; stir until cream cheese is completely melted and mixture is well blended. Add next 4 ingredients; mix well.

2. **POUR** into 13×9-inch pan sprayed with cooking spray; top with Cheddar.

3. **BAKE** 40 min. or until golden brown. Cool slightly.

SERVING SUGGESTION:
This dish is versatile enough to pair with your favorite barbecued meat, beef stew, chicken soup or even chili.

SUBSTITUTE:
Prepare using PHILADELPHIA Neufchâtel Cheese.

SPECIAL EXTRA:
Add 2 sliced green onions along with the corns, muffin mix and eggs.

MEXICAN-STYLE CORN SOUFFLE:
Prepare as directed, substituting 1 can (11 oz.) whole kernel corn with chopped red and green peppers for the plain whole kernel corn.

creamy veggies

PREP: 5 min. | TOTAL: 18 min. | MAKES: 5 servings.

▶ what you need!

1 pkg. (16 oz.) frozen mixed vegetables (California mix)

¼ lb. (4 oz.) VELVEETA 2% Milk Pasteurized Prepared Cheese Product, cut into ½-inch cubes

4 oz. (½ of 8-oz. pkg.) PHILADELPHIA Fat Free Cream Cheese, cubed

▶ make it!

1. **LAYER** ingredients in 1½-qt. microwaveable dish; cover with waxed paper.

2. **MICROWAVE** on HIGH 13 min. or until heated through, turning dish after 7 min.

3. **STIR** until well blended.

USE YOUR OVEN:
Layer ingredients in 1½-qt. casserole. Bake at 350°F for 55 min. or until heated through. Stir until well blended.

NUTRITION BONUS:
This low-fat side dish is a delicious way to eat your vegetables. Not only are the vegetables a good source of both vitamins A and C, but the cheese also provides calcium.

crispy-topped creamy spinach

PREP: 10 min. | TOTAL: 35 min. | MAKES: 12 servings.

▶ what you need!

2 pkg. (10 oz. each) frozen chopped spinach, thawed, well drained

1 tub (8 oz.) PHILADELPHIA Chive & Onion Cream Cheese Spread

½ cup KRAFT Ranch Dressing

2 eggs, beaten

1½ cups KRAFT Shredded Cheddar Cheese, divided

24 RITZ Crackers, crushed (about 1 cup), divided

▶ make it!

HEAT oven to 375°F.

1. **MIX** first 4 ingredients in large bowl until well blended. Stir in ¾ cup Cheddar and ½ cup cracker crumbs.

2. **SPOON** into greased 2-qt. casserole; top with remaining Cheddar and crumbs.

3. **BAKE** 20 to 25 min. or until casserole is heated through and cheese is melted.

HEALTHY LIVING:
Counting calories? Save 50 calories and 8 grams of fat per serving by preparing with PHILADELPHIA Chive & Onion ⅓ Less Fat than Cream Cheese, KRAFT Light Ranch Dressing, KRAFT 2% Milk Shredded Cheddar Cheese and RITZ Reduced Fat Crackers.

broccoli & cauliflower supreme

PREP: 25 min. | MAKES: 6 servings.

▶ what you need!

4 oz. (½ of 8-oz. pkg.) PHILADELPHIA Fat Free Cream Cheese, cubed

¼ cup KRAFT FREE Peppercorn Ranch Dressing

1 Tbsp. GREY POUPON Dijon Mustard

1½ bunches broccoli, cut into florets (about 6 cups), steamed, drained

½ head cauliflower, cut into florets (about 3 cups), steamed, drained

12 RITZ Reduced Fat Crackers, crushed (about ½ cup)

▶ make it!

1. **MICROWAVE** cream cheese, dressing and mustard in medium microwaveable bowl on HIGH 30 to 45 sec. or until cream cheese is softened and sauce is heated through. Stir until cream cheese is completely melted and sauce is well blended.

2. **COMBINE** vegetables in large bowl. Add sauce; toss until vegetables are evenly coated.

3. **TRANSFER** to serving bowl; top with cracker crumbs.

SUBSTITUTE:
Prepare using frozen broccoli and cauliflower florets.

NUTRITION BONUS:
Delight your family with this creamy and delicious, yet low-fat side dish that is high in both vitamins A and C from the broccoli.

creamy vegetable bake

PREP: 20 min. | TOTAL: 50 min. | MAKES: 10 servings, ¾ cup each.

▶ what you need!

1 pkg. (8 oz.) PHILADELPHIA Cream Cheese, softened

⅓ cup milk

¼ cup KRAFT Grated Parmesan Cheese

1 tsp. dried basil leaves

4 large carrots, diagonally sliced

½ lb. sugar snap peas

½ lb. fresh asparagus, cut into 1-inch lengths

1 large red bell pepper, chopped

1 pkg. (6 oz.) STOVE TOP Stuffing Mix for Chicken

▶ make it!

HEAT oven to 350°F.

1. **MICROWAVE** cream cheese and milk in large microwaveable bowl on HIGH 1 min. or until cream cheese is melted and mixture is blended when stirred. Add Parmesan and basil; stir until blended. Add vegetables; toss to coat.

2. **SPOON** into greased 13×9-inch baking dish. Prepare stuffing as directed on package; spoon over vegetable mixture.

3. **BAKE** 30 min. or until golden brown.

SUBSTITUTE:
Prepare using PHILADELPHIA Neufchâtel Cheese.

HOW TO SELECT SUGAR SNAP PEAS:
Sugar snap peas are a cross between the common English pea and snow peas. Both the pod and the peas inside are edible. Choose pods that are plump, crisp and bright green. Before using, snap off the stem ends, pulling to remove any strings.

zucchini with parmesan sauce

PREP: 10 min. | **TOTAL: 17 min.** | **MAKES: 8 servings.**

▶ what you need!

3 zucchini (1 lb.), cut diagonally into ½-inch-thick slices

2 yellow squash, cut diagonally into ½-inch-thick slices

1 red onion, cut into wedges

1 Tbsp. oil

1 tub (8 oz.) PHILADELPHIA Chive & Onion Cream Cheese Spread

⅓ cup fat-free milk

¼ cup KRAFT Grated Parmesan Cheese

¼ tsp. herb and spice blend seasoning

▶ make it!

1. **COOK** and stir vegetables in hot oil in large skillet 5 to 7 min. or until crisp-tender.

2. **MEANWHILE,** place remaining ingredients in small saucepan; cook on low heat until cream cheese spread is completely melted and mixture is well blended and heated through, stirring occasionally.

3. **SERVE** sauce over vegetables.

HEALTHY LIVING:
Save 4 grams of fat per serving by preparing with PHILADELPHIA Chive & Onion ⅓ Less Fat than Cream Cheese.

easy risotto with bacon & peas

PREP: 10 min. | COOK: 30 min. | TOTAL: 40 min. | MAKES: 6 servings, 1 cup each.

▶ what you need!

6 slices OSCAR MAYER Bacon, cut into 1-inch pieces

1 onion, chopped

1½ cups medium grain rice, uncooked

2 cloves garlic, minced

3 cans (15 oz. each) chicken broth

4 oz. (½ of 8-oz. pkg.) PHILADELPHIA Cream Cheese, cubed

1 cup frozen peas, thawed

2 Tbsp. chopped fresh parsley

2 Tbsp. KRAFT Grated Parmesan Cheese, divided

▶ make it!

1. **COOK** bacon and onions in large skillet on medium-high heat 5 min. or just until bacon is crisp, stirring occasionally.

2. **ADD** rice and garlic; cook 3 min. or until rice is opaque, stirring frequently. Gradually add ½ can broth, cook and stir 3 min. or until broth is completely absorbed. Repeat with remaining broth, adding the cream cheese with the last addition of broth and cooking 5 min. or until the cream cheese is completely melted and mixture is well blended.

3. **STIR** in peas; cook 2 min. or until peas are heated through, stirring occasionally. Remove from heat. Stir in parsley and 1 Tbsp. Parmesan. Serve topped with remaining Parmesan.

SUBSTITUTE:
Prepare using fat-free reduced-sodium chicken broth.

SERVING SUGGESTION:
Serve with hot crusty bread and a mixed green salad topped with your favorite KRAFT Dressing.

cheesy rice & corn casserole

PREP: 10 min. | TOTAL: 35 min. | MAKES: 8 servings, ½ cup each.

▸ what you need!

½ cup (½ of 8-oz. tub) PHILADELPHIA Chive & Onion Cream Cheese Spread

1 egg

2 cups cooked instant white rice

1 can (15¼ oz.) corn with red and green bell peppers, drained

1 cup KRAFT Mexican Style Finely Shredded Four Cheese, divided

2 Tbsp. chopped fresh cilantro

▸ make it!

HEAT oven to 375°F.

1. **MIX** cream cheese spread and egg in large bowl until well blended. Stir in rice, corn, ¾ cup shredded cheese and cilantro.

2. **POUR** into greased 1½-qt. casserole; top with remaining shredded cheese.

3. **BAKE** 20 to 25 min. or until is casserole is heated through and cheese is melted.

SPECIAL EXTRA:
Add 1 to 2 tsp. ground cumin for more Mexican flavor.

index

20-minute skillet salmon 192

B

baked crab rangoon 120

baked triple-veggie dip... 130

banana split cake 40

banana-sour cream cake 68

beef

creamy roast beef sandwiches 216

easy shepherd's pie 160

skillet beef picadillo with walnut sauce.................... 190

spaghetti with zesty bolognese 150

stuffed fiesta burgers... 210

berry-berry cake 72

broccoli & cauliflower supreme 240

C

cappuccino cheesecake.. 34

caramel-nut cheesecake... 18

cheesecake

cappuccino cheesecake 34

caramel-nut cheesecake 18

chocolate bliss cheesecake 28

double-layer pumpkin cheesecake 82

fruity cheesecake.. 16

layered strawberry cheesecake bowl 50

lemon pudding cheesecake 30

OREO chocolate cheesecake 36

PHILADELPHIA 3-STEP key lime
cheesecake 86

PHILADELPHIA chocolate-vanilla swirl
cheesecake 20

PHILADELPHIA classic cheesecake........................... 6

PHILADELPHIA double-chocolate
cheesecake 24

PHILADELPHIA "fruit smoothie" no-bake
cheesecake 58

PHILADELPHIA new york cheesecake........................ 22

PHILADELPHIA new york-style sour
cream-topped cheesecake 12

PHILADELPHIA new york-style strawberry
swirl cheesecake... 10

PHILADELPHIA peaches 'n cream no-bake
cheesecake 62

PHILLY brownie cheesecake 14

pumpkin swirl cheesecake 8

rocky road no-bake cheesecake 60

scrumptious apple-pecan
cheesecake 32

ultimate turtle cheesecake 26

cheese & bacon jalapeño rellenos 138

cheesy chicken tostadas 182

cheesy hot crab and red pepper spread.................. 134

cheesy rice & corn casserole 248

cheesy spinach and bacon dip 128

chicken & poultry

cheesy chicken tostadas... 182

chicken in creamy pan sauce 172

chicken parmesan bundles 170

creamy chicken pot pie... 164

creamy corn and turkey soup 200

creamy pasta primavera 148

creamy rice, chicken & spinach dinner.................... 176

creamy thai green curry chicken & rice................... 184

creamy tomato and chicken spaghetti.................... 152

farmhouse chicken dinner 178

favorite topped deviled eggs................................... 116

fiesta chicken enchiladas... 174

mexican chicken casserole 162

parmesan-crusted chicken in cream sauce 168

santa fe chicken fajita soup 204

south-of-the-border chicken & pasta skillet............. 156

tandoori chicken kabobs 166

three-cheese chicken penne pasta bake 158

turkey peppercorn ranch bites 118

tuscan chicken simmer 180

chicken in creamy pan sauce................................... 172

chicken parmesan bundles 170

chocolate & peanut butter ribbon dessert 44

chocolate bliss cheesecake.. 28

chocolate mousse torte 54

chocolate ribbon pie... 64

cinnamon toast "blinis".. 46

clam chowder 208

corn souffle 234

cream cheese flan... 48

cream cheese-bacon crescents............................... 124

creamy broccoli soup 202

creamy chicken pot pie... 164

creamy corn and turkey soup................................... 200

creamy crab and red pepper spread 108

creamy lemon squares 76

creamy pasta primavera.. 148

creamy rice, chicken & spinach dinner...................... 176

creamy roast beef sandwiches................................. 216

creamy thai green curry chicken & rice 184

creamy tomato and chicken spaghetti 152

creamy vegetable bake... 242

creamy veggies 236

crispy-topped creamy spinach 238

"croque monsieur" 198

crust topped broccoli

   cheese bake.. 232

cucumber roulades.. 90

curried pork and noodles 188

D

double-layer pumpkin cheesecake 82

E

easy cheesy scalloped potatoes 228

easy risotto with bacon & peas................................. 246

easy shepherd's pie.. 160

easy-bake cheese & pesto 140

F

farmhouse chicken dinner.. 178

fast & easy tiramisu.. 56

favorite topped deviled eggs 116

fiesta chicken enchiladas 174

fish & seafood

   20-minute skillet salmon... 192

baked crab rangoon.. 120

cheesy hot crab and red pepper spread 134

clam chowder.. 208

creamy crab and red pepper spread..................... 108

cucumber roulades 90

fish in roasted red pepper sauce 194

PHILLY shrimp cocktail dip.................................. 104

shrimp-in-love pasta... 146

swordfish with leek cream 196

terrific tuna melt.. 214

fish in roasted red pepper sauce 194

five-layer italian dip.. 136

flavor-infused cream cheese
   nibbles 102

freestyle apple tart 84

fruity cheesecake 16

G

garden vegetable grill sandwich................................ 218

garlic mashed potatoes 226

grandma's pound cake 70

H

heavenly ham roll-ups... 142

L

layered strawberry cheesecake bowl 50

lemon pudding cheesecake 30

M

make-ahead spinach phyllo roll-ups 126

mashed potato layer bake 222

mexican chicken casserole 162

mexican layered dip 96

mini cream cheese and pepper jelly phyllo cups 144

mini florentine cups 132

N

new potatoes in dill cream sauce 220

O

oat-topped sweet potato crisp 224

OREO chocolate cheesecake 36

P

parmesan-crusted chicken in cream sauce 168

peanut butter cup pie 88

pecan tassies 78

pesto crostini 106

PHILADELPHIA 3-STEP key lime cheesecake 86

PHILADELPHIA chocolate-vanilla swirl cheesecake 20

PHILADELPHIA classic cheesecake 6

PHILADELPHIA creamy salsa dip 110

PHILADELPHIA dessert dip 92

PHILADELPHIA double-chocolate cheesecake 24

PHILADELPHIA "fruit smoothie" no-bake
cheesecake 58

PHILADELPHIA marble brownies 80

PHILADELPHIA new york cheesecake 22

PHILADELPHIA new york-style sour cream-topped
cheesecake 12

PHILADELPHIA new york-style strawberry swirl
cheesecake 10

PHILADELPHIA peaches 'n cream no-bake
cheesecake 62

PHILADELPHIA tuscan dip 98

PHILLY brownie cheesecake 14

PHILLY mediterranean dip 112

PHILLY shrimp cocktail dip 104

pork

cheese & bacon jalapeño rellenos 138

cheesy spinach and bacon dip 128

clam chowder 208

cream cheese-bacon crescents 124

"croque monsieur" 198

curried pork and noodles 188

easy cheesy scalloped potatoes............................228

easy risotto with bacon & peas 246

heavenly ham roll-ups 142

mini florentine cups 132

quick pasta carbonara...154

roast pork tenderloin supper................................186

potato leek soup 206

pumpkin swirl cheesecake.......................................8

quick pasta carbonara 154

R

red velvet cupcakes..74

roast pork tenderloin supper.................................186

rocky road no-bake cheesecake 60

S

salsa roll-ups..100

santa fe chicken fajita soup 204

savory parmesan bites...122

scrumptious apple-pecan cheesecake......................32

shortcut carrot cake..66

shrimp-in-love pasta 146

skillet beef picadillo with walnut sauce 190

south-of-the-border chicken & pasta skillet 156

spaghetti with zesty bolognese..............................150

spring veggie pizza appetizer................................114

strawberry freeze 38

striped delight..42

stuffed fiesta burgers 210

sun-dried tomato & garlic dip 94

swordfish with leek cream.....................................196

T

tandoori chicken kabobs.......................................166

terrific tuna melt 214

three-cheese chicken penne pasta bake 158

turkey peppercorn ranch bites...............................118

tuscan chicken simmer 180

twice-baked sweet potatoes 230

U

ultimate turtle cheesecake......................................26

W

white chocolate-raspberry torte 52

wrapped veggie sandwich 212

Z

zucchini with parmesan sauce 244

METRIC CONVERSION CHART

VOLUME MEASUREMENTS (dry)

⅛ teaspoon = 0.5 mL
¼ teaspoon = 1 mL
½ teaspoon = 2 mL
¾ teaspoon = 4 mL
1 teaspoon = 5 mL
1 tablespoon = 15 mL
2 tablespoons = 30 mL
¼ cup = 60 mL
⅓ cup = 75 mL
½ cup = 125 mL
⅔ cup = 150 mL
¾ cup = 175 mL
1 cup = 250 mL
2 cups = 1 pint = 500 mL
3 cups = 750 mL
4 cups = 1 quart = 1 L

VOLUME MEASUREMENTS (fluid)

1 fluid ounce (2 tablespoons) = 30 mL
4 fluid ounces (½ cup) = 125 mL
8 fluid ounces (1 cup) = 250 mL
12 fluid ounces (1½ cups) = 375 mL
16 fluid ounces (2 cups) = 500 mL

WEIGHTS (mass)

½ ounce = 15 g
1 ounce = 30 g
3 ounces = 90 g
4 ounces = 120 g
8 ounces = 225 g
10 ounces = 285 g
12 ounces = 360 g
16 ounces = 1 pound = 450 g

DIMENSIONS

1/16 inch = 2 mm
⅛ inch = 3 mm
¼ inch = 6 mm
½ inch = 1.5 cm
¾ inch = 2 cm
1 inch = 2.5 cm

OVEN TEMPERATURES

250°F = 120°C
275°F = 140°C
300°F = 150°C
325°F = 160°C
350°F = 180°C
375°F = 190°C
400°F = 200°C
425°F = 220°C
450°F = 230°C

BAKING PAN SIZES

Utensil	Size in Inches/Quarts	Metric Volume	Size in Centimeters
Baking or Cake Pan (square or rectangular)	8×8×2	2 L	20×20×5
	9×9×2	2.5 L	23×23×5
	12×8×2	3 L	30×20×5
	13×9×2	3.5 L	33×23×5
Loaf Pan	8×4×3	1.5 L	20×10×7
	9×5×3	2 L	23×13×7
Round Layer Cake Pan	8×1½	1.2 L	20×4
	9×1½	1.5 L	23×4
Pie Plate	8×1¼	750 mL	20×3
	9×1¼	1 L	23×3
Baking Dish or Casserole	1 quart	1 L	—
	1½ quarts	1.5 L	—
	2 quarts	2 L	—